'Twixt
Twelve and
Twenty

To

P. Douglas Barnes

From

Mother + Dad

Christmas
December 25, 1958

Books

are keys to wisdom's
treasure;
Books are paths
that upward lead;
Books are gates
to lands of pleasure
Books are friends,
Come, let us read

P. Douglas Barnes

'Twixt
Twelve and
Twenty

by

PAT BOONE

PRENTICE-HALL, INC., Englewood Cliffs, N. J.

Fourth printing .... December, 1958

© 1958 by PRENTICE-HALL, INC., Englewood Cliffs, N. J.

COPYRIGHT UNDER INTERNATIONAL AND PAN-AMERICAN
COPYRIGHT CONVENTIONS

Library of Congress Catalog Card Number 58-14447

Printed in the United States of America

93499

Acknowledgements

The value of teamwork was one of the great things I learned during my teen-age years. I know from experience that you can't cut a record without a composer, an arranger, an orchestra, plus a whole slew of technicians. You can't produce a TV show or a movie without directors, cameramen, electricians, and a host of other specialists.

I had thought, though, that writing was different—the exception. But I found it wasn't. To write this, my first book, I needed and got a lot of help and I'd like to take this opportunity to say thanks to my "team."

To my wife, Shirley, who didn't let the chillun draw on my papers or play the piano while I was writing, and who contributed her best ideas toward the "woman's angle."

To my co-manager, Jack Spina, for keeping my nose to the grindstone (or typewriter, in this case) and cheering me on when I got discouraged.

To my two teen-age technical advisors, Kristen Dare and Joan Montgomery, for reading and re-reading these chapters to make sure they made sense (and occasionally correcting my punctuation!).

To Elaine St. Johns for her help in organizing and presenting the stuff.

To Arthur Godfrey and Ted Mack, who believe so strongly in young people's dreams.

To Monroe Stearns of Prentice-Hall for his editorial advice.

And particularly, to you, my friends out there in Teen-age Land, for the continual inspiration you have given me. If this book serves no other purpose, it at least offers a chance to say a special "thanks a million" to every one of you who have let me into your hearts and homes—and helped my *best* dreams come true!

Contents

Contents

Introduction

Hi, _____: Please write your name in here because this book is dedicated to you, and has been written for you.

In case we haven't been formally introduced, I'm Pat Boone. I sing. Right here I know you're wondering why, if I'm a singer, I don't stick to music instead of trying to write a book. Well, the answer is simple. It's *you*. I wanted a chance to talk to you personally, a just-between-us-two sort of talk with no one else (especially any grown-ups) around. And this is the best way I could think of to do it.

Why do I want to talk to you?

Well, I was sitting in my dressing room in Hollywood a while back after we had just finished making a picture, and I had just finished my umpteen hundredth interview and answered my umpteen thousandth question about teen-agers in general and myself in particular. A very nice columnist who writes for a lot of newspapers had asked the questions and taken notes like crazy and now that he was gone I sat there thinking how odd it was that five years ago when I was actually in the teen-age no one, but no one (except Shirley and I married her) seemed to care much what I thought about anything. Then suddenly, almost overnight, some of you began to buy my records—what a nice feeling!—and then a lot of people seemed interested; writers, reporters, parents, teachers, youth authorities, our milk man, his brother-in-law who is a juvenile police officer, all wanted to know what I thought about *you.*

Did I think our generation was Lost? Beat? Angry? Did *I* personally think *you* personally ate the right kind of food? Wore too much lipstick? Paid enough attention to your studies? Wore too many petticoats? Had too much freedom? How do *I* think *you* feel about haircuts, dating, homework, religion, parents, teachers? Would all of you grow up to be witch doctors or purple people eaters? Or was there hope that our generation could be really a part of the human race?

Pretty consistently I was reminded of the man who was interviewed on his hundredth birthday and asked if he thought the younger generation was going to the dogs. "Yes, sir!" he said. "I been thinkin' that for fifty years. . . ." (which means about three successive generations lost to the dogs!) But of course it wouldn't have been polite for me to give flip answers to serious questions even if I thought some of them a little silly and besides, thank you very much, I've got seventy-six years to go before I qualify as that kind of an authority. I fully expect to make it, but I do need a little time!

But what kind of an authority was I, anyhow? You can imagine how amazed you'd be if suddenly everyone began to ask you those kinds of things and then listen and write down what you said. I don't mind admitting that it embarrassed me. I would hear myself holding forth and it would sound silly and I'd think: "Pat Boone, you're talking too much. Quit yaking and get back to singing." And then I thought, "But why are they asking me, anyhow?" And the best answer I could think of was that they were maybe trying to understand us better, so they could help us more, and because so short a time ago I was one of you, they hoped I could remember and understand.

Well, on that score I am an expert. I do remember very

well! And I do understand! So the best I could do was answer as honestly as I knew how; then the writers would go off and explain us to the adults; and maybe somehow, sometimes, somewhere, it would help a little. But they didn't seem to write very often for the very people I wanted to help most— *you*, your best boy friend, your best girl friend, that goof ball next door, the poor kid who has to stay after school, all of you standing now somewhere 'twixt twelve and twenty who are, in a very special way, my good buddies and special girl friends.

If anybody has a right to know what I remember, what I understand, what I learned and how I learned it during my teen-age years, the price I paid and the mistakes I made, it's you. After the interviewer left, while sitting there in my dressing room with some of your letters on my table, I thought that since I'd finished college, since the homework pressure had eased off, I'd take time off and try to write these things for you myself.

That's exactly where, when, and how, this book was begun. And what did I hope we could talk about? Well, your letters asked a lot of questions, and although I tried to answer each one, I never really had the time or space to do it the way I wanted to. Those brief answers just never covered all the things I wanted to say. For instance, in one way or another, and sometimes just like this, you'd ask me: "What *is* Life all about?" And I'd answer the best way I could in a short space. I'd say: "Life, my friend, is terrific. Don't you ever back away from it . . . or be afraid of it . . . or let it get you down." But what I'd really like to have done was order us both a cold coke (or Seven-Up), and sit back and say, "Well, now that you *ask*, we ought to talk things over—a lot of things." I, myself, like the way the Walrus put it in Through the Looking Glass:

> "The time has come," the Walrus said,
> "To talk of many things:

Of shoes—and ships—and sealing wax—
Of cabbages—and kings—
And why the sea is boiling hot—
And whether pigs have wings."

Because that's the honest answer to what life is all about
—many, many things. It's about dating, and going steady, and
falling in love; getting married and having children. It's
about making friends, and learning things; making mistakes,
falling down, getting bruised, picking yourself up and starting all over again. It's about the things you eat, and the things
you wear, the games you play, the things you do, the things
you think, working, playing, finding your special talent,
making the most of yourself so that you can enjoy it *all*. It's
about music, books, pictures, and politics, and getting along
with the guy next door, with teachers, with parents (and
some day a boss and an in-law or two!).

It's about how to be kind, happy, successful.

It's about you and your relationship to God!

It's all these things and many others that make life terrific
and they are the things I thought we'd discuss. Dr. Louis L.
Mann once said: "By the time we appreciate how important
youth is, youth isn't." I want to help you to understand how
important it is right now. How important you are right now!
How vital the choices are that you make today. How you can
really enjoy life this minute, and all the minutes to come!

Well—here it is, my book, dedicated to you. It's not a clas-
sic. It will have shortcomings. I can't guarantee my literary
style, only my intentions. I have tried to be completely honest, to share with you my faith, hopes, dreams, experiences
(and faults!) not with the idea of making you a whole lot better (I'm not in the least worried about your being "good"
. . . I know you . . . I've read your letters, I know the stuff
you're made of, and it's good goods already) but in the hope
of making you a little bit happier.

I may not be the wisest, or the oldest, or the most experienced person you know. But you will not find anyone, any-where, who has a more sincere desire to see you climb that ladder of seven teen-age years with real enjoyment and arrive up here in the adult world ready for a happy, successful life.

So pull up your chair, pretend I just offered you an all-day straw for that coke, and let's talk. We have a lot to say to each other!

Your boy,

PAT BOONE

Hollywood, California

1

A Great Adventure

In my family we have what we call "why" babies. I was one of them myself.

From the time I could talk I asked questions. "Why does grass grow right side up?" "Why don't elephants have pouches like kangaroos?" "Why do I have to wait a year for Christmas?" "Why can't I have a whole pie all to myself?"

Now that I have four babies of my own, I've discovered this habit isn't unusual. You probably asked questions, too. And I suppose you found out that, when the question made sense, you got an answer. And when it didn't, you were rightfully ignored.

The point I'm making is that, up to a certain age, all the questions had to do with things around me—like grass, and Christmas, and elephants. If they were about me personally, they usually concerned my stomach or something I wanted.

Then, in the sixth grade, our teacher, who had been trying to pound facts about American inventions into our heads, asked a question: "Can you name something of importance that didn't exist fifty years ago?"

And a bright girl in the back of the room said: "Me!"

She got a real big laugh (and some extra homework), but it also started me thinking. Fifty years ago I wasn't. Now I am. And whether or not that was important to anyone in the world besides my family, it was certainly important to me. This idea launched me on a whole new set of questions. Who was I? Where did I come from? Where was I going? Why was I born? Did life have a meaning?

I didn't know it then, but with this dawning awareness I was about to enter a sort of Never-Never-Land. The teen age was knocking at my front door. And I think that's the way it happens to most of us. We begin to try to get answers to these very large questions. And the answers we come up with form the principles by which we run our later lives. They form our characters. They guide our actions. From this point on we begin to put away the dolls and sling-shots and struggle to become adults.

These seven teen-age years are a great adventure. They're tremendously important. And we can be certain sure of one thing: nobody ignores us any more.

The fact is that suddenly everyone wants to answer our questions. Friend and foe. Parent and teacher. Church members and public committees. The wise and the unwise. There are books and columns and lectures by perfect strangers who are happy to tell us all they know, to tell us what to do and how to do it. How to dress. How to bathe. How to succeed. How to make friends. How to snare a worthwhile husband or wife.

The result, for a while, can be utter confusion. I know I felt exactly like the man whose wife asked him to copy a radio recipe. He tuned in two stations at once, one giving the recipe, the other setting up exercises. This is what he took down:

"Hands on hips, place one cup of flour on your shoulder, raise knees and depress toes; mix thoroughly in one-half cup of milk, repeat six times. Inhale quickly one-half teaspoon of baking powder, lower the legs and mash two hard-boiled eggs in a sieve; exhale breath naturally and sift in a bowl. Attention! Lie flat on the floor and roll in whites of two eggs backward and forward until it comes to a boil. In ten minutes remove from fire and rub smartly with a rough towel. Breathe naturally, dress in warm flannels and serve with tomato soup."

It couldn't be done. There was too much to remember, too many places to get crossed up, too much contradictory advice. It wasn't meant to confuse. All of it was very well intended. Most advice is. But that didn't help me. What was I to do?

Without my realizing it, I began to follow a sound piece of advice from the Bible: "Prove all things. Hold fast that which is good."

Obviously I couldn't prove everything in a few short years. But I found that it was necessary for me to sort through some of this free wisdom and then experiment a little. Was it true for me? It would be a very wonderful thing if we could profit one hundred percent by the experience of others. Then we wouldn't have to make any mistakes. But you wonder how, if our elders had done exactly that, they would have got the experience they want to pass on to us.

It seems to me that the greatest help I got was from people who briefed me on what lay ahead and offered their experience as a guide. They then suggested that, instead of doing what they said just because they said it, I find out whether it was true.

Your mother says, "That fire is hot. If you touch it, it will burn you." To hear her, you would think she had touched it herself. And at some point, you touch it yourself. It burns. Now right there, you're willing to stop. She told you the truth. She is a reliable source. Her stock goes up and you are willing to trust her word a little more next time.

Of course, there are those who will try again tomorrow to see if fire is as hot Saturday as it was Friday. Then people say, "Now there's a stubborn child. He'll have to learn the hard way." And this is true, too. But if the child goes right on touching the fire, they say, "That child's not all there." And this can be tragically correct.

For those of us who are not so stubborn, who have all our marbles, I believe the teen age can be a really great experience. It was for me. You won't get through it without making mistakes. That's out of the question. But perhaps, if I share some of mine with you, as well as some of the rules I found for coming out ahead, you can get through with only a slight scald where you might have got a third degree burn.

As teen-agers we need more than advice and answers to our questions. We need understanding. We need sympathy. We need affection. Same as people! Since I myself have only traveled four short years beyond the world that exists between childhood and being an adult, I find that when your letters come in I can feel exactly what you feel. I can sympathize with your hopes and dreams and encourage you because only a few years ago all I had were hopes and dreams. I sympathize with your smarts, too, because I still feel the sting. And besides that, I'm kind of partial to you.

I know you have what it takes, with a little help, to be the really wonderful, happy, person God intended you to be. It may be that you're being offered that help right now and I can show you a way to accept it. Maybe you are not being offered it, and so my little bit will come in handy. Or maybe you are confused and I can show you how I found a straight line to travel.

But remember, it isn't true because I say it. "Prove all things. Hold fast that which is good."

"Twice on Sunday and once in the middle of the week"

Well, there I was . . . twelve years old. On the threshold of the teens, with a good deal of experience about the difference 'twixt right and wrong. In our family this difference was called to our attention by spanking.

My earliest recollection is of church, but it's hardly a pious memory. Although I was born in Jacksonville, Florida, and

Mama started totin' me to church twice on Sunday and once in the middle of the week when I was six weeks old, we had moved to Donelson, Tennessee, before I had any clear idea of what was going on. In the little rural church in Donelson I can distinctly recall marching up the aisle with my younger brother Nick to the front row where Mama and Daddy always sat; and then, right in the middle of the sermon, being marched down the aisle again. The entire congregation of one hundred or so people knew where Mama was taking me. And I *knew* they knew. I was being hustled out front to be blistered!

From then until I was six I don't remember sitting all the way through a service.

It was "wrong" to talk, laugh, giggle, or get so carried away that I made signs to a pal across the church during the sermon. "You mustn't do anything at all to distract people in church," my mother said. "They are there on important business."

And when we did what was "wrong," she called our attention to it at the exact moment of the error. If it was something really bad, Daddy took over when he got home. I know there's a lot of pros and cons on the subject of spanking, but one of the most successful dog trainers in Hollywood once explained the psychology of it in a way that makes sense to me. He didn't "beat" his dogs any more than Mama "beat" us. "It is a question of getting their *attention*" he said. "The easiest way to get the full attention of a child or a puppy is with a sharp crack across the bustle."

He also explained that the child and the dog begin to associate certain misdeeds with an immediate unpleasant sensation, and thus Mama was quite sound in her on-the-spot attention-getters. It's the principle of cause and effect!

Whether we've been spanked or not when we arrive at the teen age is entirely out of our hands. If we have been spanked, our reaction will determine whether we become "spanking" parents. It is simply one of the methods used to

help children distinguish right from wrong at an early age.
And of course there are spankings—and spankings. There is
the delayed spanking that sets in when you're too old to go
across Mama's knee and have to wait until you get you home
and lean over the bathtub. There is the angry spanking, and
the loving spanking. My mother never gave "loving" spankings. I wouldn't know what they were. But hers weren't angry either; they were intelligent and they were just.

I'll never forgive myself for one thing. I myself found the
instrument of our torture at the age of four in the back yard
at Donelson. It was a sewing machine belt, and it has hung
in our bathroom ever since! The reason is that although my
youngest sister, Judy, is now fifteen, Mother says, "If you
were thirty-five and I thought you needed it, I would still
spank you." You know what? I believe her!

If you've never had your share of this type of teaching,
you don't know what you're missing. But you'll still find
that you cannot arrive at the teen-age threshold without
gaining a certain idea of what is socially acceptable. Your
parents may have used other methods. They may not have
bothered. But if they didn't, someone else did: a teacher, a
policeman, the neighbors, good friends—even, I regret to
say, your so-called enemies.

The question is, did it take? What do we do with what we
are taught?

Spanking worked wonders in my case. In Donelson I am
still remembered as "the little boy Mrs. Boone had to take
out every Sunday," while in Nashville, Tennessee, where we
moved when I was six, I am "that little boy who was such a
little gentleman in the front row." Took six years, but it
worked! Looking back, there seems to be every indication
that I was a "stubborn" child. Surely I carried on more experimenting than should have been necessary.

The lesson once learned, however, had a further and very
lasting effect. Mama had conditioned me to pay attention, to
control my body so that my mind was ready to follow what

was being said. However this lesson is learned, it's a good one. It sure came in handy in school, I'll say that. And what I heard in church, once I learned to listen, helped me to establish the principles that carried me through the teen years. If nobody teaches this lesson to you, it's one I strongly recommend you learn for yourself.

Now, this brings us back to the point of when and how we approach our teen-age years. Let's admit that most of us have picked up, from some source or another, a pretty good idea of right and wrong conduct. But one day, when we're eleven, or twelve, or thirteen, we begin to ask those other questions. Who am I? What is my purpose in life? We put away dolls and toy soldiers and begin to look at real live babies and flesh-and-blood soldiers and wonder: What lies ahead? Will I be happy? Will I be rich? Whom will I marry? Will there be rainbows day after day?

And we don't take "Whatever will be will be" for an answer, because it isn't true. We sense that we have a part in shaping "whatever will be." Now it becomes important that we learn about right and wrong thinking, right and wrong aims and desires. We begin to choose for ourselves what sort of people we'll be, what we'll learn, what we'll do.

The outward guidance of sewing machine belts and standing in the corner gets more scarce, and we struggle to develop inner guidance of our own. Because, pretty soon, there's going to be no passing the buck to anyone else for our mistakes.

It's fair to evaluate what you have learned thus far. In fact it's necessary. At this point we're all a little like the boy who borrowed a book on "Child Training" from the lady next door. His mother laughed. "Do you find it amusing?" she asked. "I'm not reading it for that," he said solemnly, "I merely wanted to see if I'd been brought up properly."

The answer to that one, if we are honest, is "yes" nine times out of ten. But if we are that tenth one, then we can and should begin to bring ourselves up. It can be done, my friend. The real challenge is to decide what the right way is and then to reach that even bigger decision to walk "that-a-way."

I don't mind admitting that I put my decision off a whole year after I knew what I had to do. And perhaps, if I tell you about that, it will help you in your own decision.

"Solitude"

When I was ten we got a cow named Rosemary. And it was my duty, as the elder son, to trudge out to the barn daily to do the milking. When I didn't want to do it, I would mutter about "cutting that old cow into little pieces," but as I got to be eleven and twelve, as I began to ask those *big* questions, I found the barn, with nobody there but Rosemary and me, a very fine place to think—and to dream. Milking, as I'm sure you know (what, you never milked a cow?) keeps your hands busy but requires very little mental effort.

I found that being alone with time to ponder and think was just as necessary as time in church, or school, or time to play. I believe that each one of us, whether we walk in the country, or lie on the beach and look at the waves, or sit cross-legged under a tree in our back yard, can gain a great deal from learning to be quiet once in a while and think things through.

So I would sit in the barn and milk that cow and think. I had this big decision to make.

Was I ready to become a Christian?

Now, some grown-ups might not understand this. They would think I went to church twice every Sunday and once in the middle of the week and sat very still in the front row. They would think that, in spite of spankings, this did not mean such a very big change for me. That I had never done anything so terrible, nor had such bad habits that I should be worried about whether I could be a good Christian.

But that's because they don't remember how seriously we take promises at that age. Or maybe they just don't understand what's involved in trying to be a good Christian.

It is true that, like most of us, I had lived a normal and fairly "good" life until then. I did all the usual things. As a direct descendant of Daniel Boone it followed that I played pioneer in the woods. And, being a modern youth, I alternated that game with being a soldier or gangster or Tarzan, swinging from ropes we suspended from tree limbs. I can't count the number of times that as a commando I captured the hill that led up from an abandoned rock quarry in our neighborhood. All harmless fun.

I think I was obedient to my parents out of love as much as by commandment. That is, when I *was* obedient. Mama is pretty terrific, a cheerful, optimistic woman, vigorous and always busy, who belongs to lots of groups and loves contests. If she's enthusiastic about a new vitamin she immediately gets the dealership so she can sell it to the whole town. She has a quick temper that flares easily and then dies down as suddenly as it burst out. Before I was born she was a registered nurse, but after that she didn't practice on anyone but her children. Believe me, that was full-time employment. As my brother came along one year to the day after I did, and then three years later Margie and four years after that Judy, we kept her pretty busy. I alone contributed by breaking my nose three times, both arms, my collarbone, one wrist, plus suffering innumerable sprains and cuts.

Mama is great fun too, and has a mind of her own. She had counted on my being a girl, "Patricia," and when I crossed her up, she named me Charles Eugene for two uncles and promptly called me "Pat." I am not at liberty to disclose the names of the uncles for whom she officially named my brother. That's his secret. But it didn't matter because she immediately called him "Nick" for the sole reason that it sounded nice with "Pat." We all thought Mama the greatest and I tell her now that she can spank me any time she likes.

Daddy is quiet, considerate, steady, prompt, hard-working, and he never considered any job beneath him. Name a virtue and my Dad has it. So it wasn't difficult to love my parents. Maybe I was luckier than a lot of kids.

But sometimes it was difficult to obey them. Also, before the moment of my big decision, it was so difficult not to fight with my little brothers and sisters that even the sewing machine strap didn't stop me. I felt it countless times for such things as burning flour sacks in the barn for absolutely no reason except that I happened to have some matches and liked to watch the smoke.

These were unquestionably "wrong" things to do. That much I had learned while meditating over Mama's knee, as she applied the strap. But there were other things I began to wonder about as I sat in my solitude in the barn with Rosemary. Now that I was aware that I was "me," I wondered if other people were "me" too. Did they have feelings and problems and dreams and hurts just as I did? Even grown-up people?

I thought about my father in particular.

We had never had an automobile-type car. Since we lived in a middle-class suburb where "everyone else had a car" we felt it keenly when we all had to ride around in our Chevy pick-up truck labeled "Boone Construction Company." In fair weather Nick and I rode on a bleacher Daddy built in the back. But if the weather was bad all six of us huddled in the cab. People laughed. It was good-natured laughter, but none the less we were very sensitive about it. I, personally, would be very self-conscious when we arrived at the large and beautiful David Lipscomb Church twice on Sunday in this improvised chariot, and utterly mortified if any of my friends saw me.

We gave Daddy a pretty bad time about it, but he never showed either ill-temper or hurt. We'd offer schemes for borrowing the money to buy that car, or selling the house. Anything to be like the others. And my father would try to make a joke of it: "Roomy . . . air-conditioned . . . everybody wants a convertible and you boys don't even have to put the top down." But we didn't think it was funny. Not we hardheads.

Now it suddenly occurred to me that this was wrong. Not by the standard of the sewing machine belt. This wasn't the sort of thing you got licked for. This was wrong according to what God expected of me. Does that sound a little Sunday-schoolish? Maybe that's good.

Through Bible reading and paying attention in church and soaking up a little of the folks' teaching, I had come to believe that the right way for me was the way Christ taught. That He had the answers to the big questions that had been bothering me.

Yet, when my brother decided to be baptized and my parents asked me if I was ready, I held back. Instead, I went out alone into the barn with Rosemary and thought some more.

"Now I know"

A very famous minister once planned a trip to Europe and his friends kidded him about bringing back a "new religion." "If you do," they teased, "it might be hard to get it through customs."

"I guess not," he laughed. "We may take it for granted that any new religion popular enough to be imported will have no duties attached."

The Church of Christ, of which my family and I are members, is not a "new religion." It's purpose is to continue the church with its faith and practice exactly as it was in the days of the Apostles. The worship meetings of the apostolic church nearly two thousand years ago were simple, sincere, joyous, and relatively informal, though reverent. And that's the way we worship. But since religion then was based on the Bible and the teachings of Jesus, it could not be without certain duties. Neither is it now.

When we're baptized we're taking a very, very, serious step. To take it, I had to be ready to devote my life to Christ. It was not merely a matter of being saved and having my sins forgiven. In other words, it's not a one-sided proposition. God doesn't intend to do it all. I had to take on the responsibilities of being a Christian. That's a tall order.

It was a way of life—not a week-end hobby.

This was going to mean a change, brother. It was going to mean more than not burning flour sacks and sitting still in church. I suspected it would put an end to teasing Daddy about the car. But it would mean more even than that. It would mean that I would have to try to be completely honest. That's tough. To do things I thought were right and to do my level best not to do things I thought were wrong, whether there was a spanking waiting to remind me or not. I would have to love my friends enough to warn them tactfully if I thought they were off base (and that's asking a lot of an eleven- or twelve-year-old), and refuse to do things a lot of my close pals did.

You can see why I hesitated, can't you? Even the temptation not to let my kid brother get ahead of me didn't alter the fact that I still had some thinking to do. To jump the gun because Nick was "ready" would have been bowing to pressure. Or doing what was expected of me. I knew it wasn't any good unless I did it because I wanted to.

Then one evening out in the barn I finally realized that for me the Bible had the answers. That the teachings of Jesus answered all the questions I was asking: Who was I? Where did I come from? Why was I born? Where am I going? That if I let Him take over, my life would definitely have a meaning.

After all, the first twelve years had flown by in a hurry. The next fifty would, too. Life is short. After that comes a real long time we call eternity. How pleasant that is depends on what we do in our short lifetime.

Now I knew! This was it.

I was baptized shortly before my thirteenth birthday.

The fact is that at that moment I had taken over the responsibility for my own conduct, using Christ's teachings as a guide or yardstick. If I tried hard to obey them and failed, I might get a slight scald. But if I kept trying I would never get a third degree burn.

I didn't become a good Christian overnight. In fact I got my last spanking when I was seventeen, a junior in high school and already going with Shirley (who is now my wife). When I came to school and said, "Guess what happened this morning? I got spanked," she didn't believe me. But I did. For getting into a row with Nick. It never mattered to Mama who started fights. She finished them with the sewing machine belt and both of us leaning over the bathtub. It had been a long time, however, since the last one, and this time neither of us cried. We were too old. That shattered Mama. Which is probably the reason that I haven't got one since, although I'm sure I've deserved them. You see, I am not what you'd call a really good Christian yet. Not the kind I'd like to be. I'm a "trying" Christian. And any of us can be that. Including you.

Trying to be a Christian doesn't hurl you by jet propulsion into the promised land. It simply means you've started on your own Pilgrim's Progress. And I don't know any better way to recommend for passing over the rough stretches of road in the teen-age adventure. It gives you a road map. It gives you goals and aims. A purpose. Rules and duties. But more than that, it gives you Someone to help you, to guide, to guard, to comfort you. This isn't a fairy tale, my friend, like Saint Nick or the Easter Bunny. God is very real. I wouldn't say this to you if I didn't know—first hand. And no matter what happens once you're traveling under His banner, you can't ever again be completely misunderstood, or lost, or alone.

2

Jam Today

What is a teen-ager? And why?

Let's take a look at that one together because I think the better we understand ourselves as we go through those years, the more we can make of them and the better we can enjoy them.

I'll say one thing: I know what we are *not*. While we are truly in-betweeners, we are not "left out." We're not separate from the human race. Not by a long shot.

I know what we *feel* like sometimes. We feel that we're set apart, shooed off together, accused as a group until we get on the defensive and deny everything like the little boy who was raiding the hen house, and, when the farmer appeared, piped up "Ain't nobody here but us chickens, Boss."

Well, what *are* we? We're a group of individuals who are making a change. *The greatest single change, physical, mental, and emotional, in the shortest period of time, that we will ever be called upon to make.*

This has some agreeable symptoms. Usually we're dreamers, romantic, and suddenly serious. The girls are getting prettier and their figures are getting womanly. The tubby boy next door shoots up into a tall, attractive youth, like my ol' buddy, Don Henley.

But there are symptoms which we all share to some degree that are not as attractive and are apt to be as painful. And I mean painful!

Teen-age symptoms

First: *Insecurity.* I remember existing in a kind of in-between world with my back toward childhood and my face toward adulthood but actually feeling that I didn't belong "no place."

You're too old to be content with a soap box car and too young to own a real one (and too poor to buy it if you could). You're too old to be satisfied playing with dolls and not old enough for the responsibilities of a real live family. Kid parties are dull because they play pin-the-tail-on-the-donkey or tag. Grown-up parties are duller because all they do is talk—or play bridge. You're dying to go on a date, but at the last minute you wish you were baby-sitting or working for your dad because you aren't sure you will be dressed properly, or know what to say, and you decide you didn't want to go anyhow.

It's a tough life! There is a lot of stress and strain as you're pulled in two directions: backward, toward childhood, by a host of yesterday's habits; and forward, toward adulthood, by a host of tomorrow's dreams. You have one foot pointed in each direction and both a little off the ground, and you feel you could tip very easily. You often slip and fall and hurt yourself—inside, where it really hurts.

The chief trouble is that we are not sure of ourselves. We tend to become shy, fearful, to ward off inferiority feelings, or mask it all with a hollow superior manner that can make us very unpleasant company.

Second: *Restlessness.* We just can't seem to settle into the moment. We feel we should be traveling faster, but we're not sure where. We flutter and flit both mentally and physically, trying to find a place to light. Time takes on a new dimension. It doesn't function by mother's voice, or school bells, or our stomachs so much now. Now time is a measure of progress, mental and emotional time, and, not understanding it, we run from it. We're impatient sometimes with ourselves, or with others. We don't know where we're going, or who we're going with, or what we want when we get there —but we're on our way! That's for sure.

THIRD: *Inconsistency.* I remember how exasperated my brother Nick was when even his voice wouldn't stay the same. He had about a three octave interplay. One minute he would squeak like a mouse and the next minute boom like a foghorn. Very interesting conversationalist. Or my sister, Margie, thinking one day that Bud was the only boy in the world and wanting to bite our mother's head off for mentioning that he was still at the sloppy clothes stage. Then, two days later when Mama said she'd seen Bud at church very neat in a new suit, Sis would say, "Oh, him!" as if he should be on a slow boat to Nowhere.

One day you're filled with enthusiasm for getting all A's and becoming an atomic scientist, and the next you've decided to retire from the world, sit under a cork tree and smell the flowers. High flown resolutions are made today— and broken tomorrow. When we sense that this is in any way "different" we become secretive. If anyone tries to make us stay on one track we're even a mite resentful. We understand ourselves. It should be easy for parents and friends to understand us. But do we? And is it?

FOURTH: *Indecision.* Let's face it. A lot of times we simply cannot make up our minds, in the most determined way. Should we or should we not ask that pretty girl for a date? Should we or should we not wear an old dress that's tried and true or a new dress Aunt Minnie sent that doesn't quite fit right? Should we go to church or should we go to a picnic? Or the heartbreaking indecision of whether we should pretend we live in a brick mansion, and then never be able to bring any friends home. Or should we let them know we live in a small frame house on the wrong side of the tracks and risk losing their friendship?

We feel very frustrated, but let any older person try to help us decide and they are likely to find that we are positive in our indecision. We don't need any help. We are a little like Sam Goldwyn, the famous Hollywood producer, who once said: "I want you to know that I am not always right—but I am never wrong."

Now, if we just let these symptoms run riot we will find we are out of balance. The changes we make will be abrupt and painful for us and everyone around us. We'll find ourselves moody, resentful, impatient, feeling either superior or inferior, living with a closed mind, a sense of loneliness, and nagging guilts and fears.

This is the hard way.

But there is an easier, happier way. Check yourself on these symptoms. Finding the ones that plague us, and usually it is a touch of all four, we can go to work on bringing ourselves back into balance or harmony again.

Sorting out values

One way I found to begin to control the three "Ins"— Insecurity, Inconsistency, Indecision—was to get my values straight. I had to ask myself questions. Why am I trying to impress people? Whom am I trying to impress? What is important to me? Where should the emphasis be—on what I have or on what I am? How do I judge other people? By whether they have a big house or whether they have a nice smile?

We can't honestly say right off the bat that we don't place the greatest importance on outward things. I know I used to think they were all-important.

Looking back, I cringe a little, because it seems silly—and even worse. You remember how badly we wanted a family car instead of a truck. Well, we got it. When I was in the eighth grade, my dad bought the most inexpensive Chevy sedan made. A small, black, two door model, with black tires and not one single accessory. But to me it was a badge of success. Now we were "like everybody else." I bragged about that car as if Queen Elizabeth had just sent us her Rolls-Royce. The first few mornings we begged Dad into driving us to school so that everyone could see us. And I even ran ahead through the back pasture, which adjoined the school playground, to alert my friends so that they would be watching for our arrival.

But do you know something? Not one of my friends liked me a bit more. And what little laughter the new car evoked was not good natured. It was superior. I honestly think they saw through me!

Even with the new car, however, I still found things to make me feel insecure. We were moderately well off, had our own comfortable house and ten acres of ground. We lived in an average suburban area and went to a suburban school. But our place was positively rural. The other houses were new, trim, with badminton courts, sleek lawns, flowering hedges. Ours was older, kind of plain, and frame. We didn't have hedges, we had fences (sort of run down); and no badminton courts, just a barn.

The barn was where Rosemary lived and Rosemary was my cross. Rosemary and the turkeys, and chickens, and pigs, and horses. We weren't gentleman farmers. We had those things because we had a big family and had to cut corners. Nicky and I each drank a gallon of milk a day. Rosemary was a necessity, not a luxury. It wasn't so much that I didn't like the animals or that I hated milking a cow. It was that we didn't live in a farming community.

These things made us different!

Of course if they had been different enough—if Rosemary had been a flying purple people eater, or even a purple cow

—I would have enjoyed that in my inconsistency. But she wasn't. This plain old bossy came to us as a calf, and we retired her when I was nineteen.

I learned a lot from Rosemary besides the value of solitude. Rosemary wouldn't stay put. She was a wanderer. You can imagine how welcome Rosemary was when she got out and went gallumphing around our fancy suburb, into yards, breaking down badminton nets, munching prize roses and, cows being cows, leaving her trail behind her! And I had to chase her.

It embarrassed me to death!

Then I would catch her on a velvety front lawn, and just as I got my hands on her, she'd take off again with me in hot pursuit, while people looked out of windows, shaking their heads either in laughter or anger.

I always knew that somebody would see me, somebody I didn't want to see me. It never seemed to fail that, as I chased her down a road, a carload of my friends (and usually the girl I was flirting with at school just then) would be coming my way.

I was well into my teens and almost six feet tall the afternoon that, sure enough, the worst happened. There went Rosemary, there was I chasing after her. Here came a car. In it was *the* girl. Joan! And beside the road was a sort of ditch. After a second of tortured indecision I hit the ditch, trying to hide. And of course *the* girl spotted me there and I looked a bigger fool than ever. You know how painful those moments can be.

The way I felt about our house was more than painful, because there was a layer of guilt spread over it like butter on bread.

I was ashamed of our house.

It looks awful set down in words like that. And it hurts to admit it. But we won't be getting anyplace if we aren't honest with ourselves and each other. Almost every teen-ager I know has been ashamed of something connected with his home or family. In my case there was less excuse than most because, while we didn't have a lot of luxuries, Mama was willing to share everything we had. She always cooked extra food and all of our friends were welcome, even the whole class. I just didn't bring anybody for a while.

Well, I was hurting. I was doing it the hard way. So now and then I did some serious thinking about the situation. Whom *was* I trying to impress? What *was* important to me? How did people judge me and how did I judge other people? Did I want to be myself or pretend to be somebody else?

I came to believe that people were not as interested in what I had or what I wore as in what I *was*. If I wasn't satisfied with that, I could go to work to change it. I decided that comparing myself with other people was not a good way to measure my own worth! If I didn't have the voice of Perry Como and the face of Clark Gable, well, I'd have to make the most of the face and voice I had. If I didn't have a badminton court and I did have a cow, then I'd face the reality and adjust to it. If we lived in an old frame house I would stop hankering after an all-glass modern one and be proud of the love and affection we had in our home.

For each one of us these evaluations will be different. We have to take stock of what we have, make friends with it, accept it. Some youngsters have only one parent. Some have none. Some face problems of financial lack, limitations, and such. This is a pattern that has been imposed upon us. We couldn't help it. When our day comes we can try to change it if we like. But for now, we have to make up our minds what we can change and what we cannot change. We have to begin to credit other people with being as kind as we are ourselves.

I found that the things that mattered most to me personally were love, people, fun, kindness, laughter, creating things. It healed me of a lot of insecurity to find out that if my cow gave people a laugh, I was doing them a favor. They liked it! If I wore the wrong shirt, nobody seemed to think less of me. My friends didn't notice my house so much as they praised Mama's cooking.

You know, I found I could make decisions more quickly if I based them on kindness, on what was right and good in the situation. I could begin to develop a consistent attitude as soon as I knew what was important to me.

The most important thing is to make up your mind what is important, what is temporary and what is lasting, what is for real and what is just a symptom of the changing teens, like Nicky's voice or my skinniness, or the roly-poly stage some of the girls at school went through.

Jam today

A lady once remarked to the Irish playwright and wit, George Bernard Shaw, that youth is a wonderful time of life. And Shaw replied, "Yes. What a crime to waste it on the young!"

When we look at one of our teen-age symptoms, restlessness, we begin to understand what Shaw meant and we can keep youth from being wasted on us.

Juanita Bartlett, executive girl in our office, wears a little locket on which is inscribed: "Jam Today." You remember where that comes from? *Through the Looking Glass,* where the White Queen told Alice she couldn't have any jam today, because "The rule is, jam tomorrow and jam yesterday— but never jam *today.*"

A wise man said that "most people are as happy as they make up their minds to be." Now, I think I am a very happy person. And the secret of it, for me, is that happiness is a thing called now. I feel so strongly about it that I'd even like to write a song with that title.

The reason it's never jam today is that most of us live yesterday or tomorrow. Older people either long for the past

or worry about the future. Today is just a hyphen in between. Ever think of that? This is as silly as the lady who
lost all her hair. "How did you lose it?" a friend asked.
"Worry," she said. "What did you worry about?" "Losing
my hair."

Teen-agers generally want to storm on into tomorrow
before they have lived today. Let me tell you a secret. Today is all you have. Tomorrow will only be another today
when it arrives. Enjoy today to the full and tomorrow will
be another day to enjoy.

One of the things that used to rub me the wrong way was
to hear an adult say to a younger person, "Act your age."
I still think the way many of them say it is insulting. That's
too bad, because it's really very good advice.

Youth *is* wonderful!

But we can spoil it or waste it. What's the hurry? What's
the big rush? You'll never be eleven, or twelve, or thirteen,
or any other teen year but once. Each day you can figure, "I
have not passed this way before . . . and I will not pass
this way again." Today is unique. Don't let its wonderful
moments go by unnoticed—and unused.

I promise you something: You will grow ahead fast
enough. The time will come when you can drive a car.
When you can date unchaperoned. Marry. Earn a living.
When you can wear spike heeled shoes or a dinner jacket.
But if you are only going to be happy when those times
come, you will never be happy. Because then you will have
the "tomorrow" habit.

I once knew a fellow who was "going to be happy" when
he could drive a car. So that day came, but by then he was
"going to be happy" when he could buy one. So he bought
one. Then he was "going to be happy" when he could better
it with a Corvette. And he actually got a Corvette. But by
then the habit had a strong hold on him. He was "going to
be happy" when a certain girl married him. He even got the

girl. Then it was a certain job, then security, then when his family was grown. I don't think he'll ever make it.

We won't go into whether it makes us a little ridiculous to be running around attempting to appear to be something we are not, because we should not make these changes based on what others will think of us. There would be no lasting value there. That's a "control" just like a spanking. But I'll tell you something. My very good friend, Bobby Morrow, says one of the reasons he won three gold medals at the Olympics is that he has never jumped the gun. Jumping the gun has penalties. Both you and I have seen some of the penalties paid by teen-agers who insist on living ahead of their physical or emotional or mental age and growth. At the worst, cars piled up. Girls' lives ruined. Boys in juvenile court. At the least, unbalanced lives, a lot of extra problems and discomfort.

You know, I think a lot of our worries and anxieties are rooted right here in this time goof, the inability to live today. And guilt, too—guilt if we haven't done today what today brought to us to do. You ask some depressed older fella, "What are you thinking of?" He says sadly, "My future." You say, "What makes your future so hopeless?" He replies, "My past!"

Yet, like us, all that he has is today.

To guard against needless worry and anxiety, to overcome restlessness, impatience, and frustration, to be happy *now* and not waste a moment of our wonderful youth, I think we should all have written somewhere, on a locket, or in our minds, or on a sign in our room! *Jam Today.*

3

Do It Yourself

What does it really mean to "grow up?"

Did you ever think it meant a kind of a Cloud Nine existence where you could run your own show in your own way? Well, 'tain't so! Remember the wisdom offered by a father whose son wanted to know: "When will I be old enough to do as I please?" And the old man replied: "I don't know. Nobody ever lived that long."

That's about the size of it.

Our physical growth—height, hands, feet (especially feet!)—is miraculously taken care of whether we cooperate or not. But the growth we have to concern ourselves with is strictly the do-it-yourself kind. To be really grown-up is to arrive at maturity.

I think we have today potentially the brightest, nicest, most advanced teen-agers ever. Such an authority as Heman G. Stark, Director of the State of California Youth Authority, agrees with this. Says Mr. Stark: "On the basis of my thirty years' experience, I'd say . . . the teen-agers of today are

stronger, smarter, more self-sufficient, and more construc-
tive than any other generation of teen-agers in history."

The big question is, is he talking about a group? Or about
you? You can ask, "Who, *us?*" Or, "Who, *me?*"

Your individual growth toward maturity is what you personally are doing to fulfill your all-round potential. The
dictionary describes maturity as "a state or quality of *full*
development."

Then a mature person will be the one who has made
the most of himself in all departments. A mature teen-ager
will be the one who is least distorted by those four teen-age
symptoms we mentioned, and can live comfortably and harmoniously with himself and the world. In other words when,
at any age, we are useful, happy, well-adjusted individuals,
able to give as much as we get—we are mature!

How about that? Isn't that a more attractive goal than
"doing as I please?" The joke is that maturity doesn't seem
to be a question of how old you are. I've known a few people
of fifty in fully-grown bodies who haven't even made a start.
And very young teen-agers who are well on their way.

For all round development I'd like to offer you a check
list I've used to help myself. Five of these points coincide
with a list used by Gale Storm. She and her husband devote
every New Year's Eve to measuring their progress and chart-
ing their goals in these major areas: Spiritual, Social, Mental,
Physical, Financial. I added one more—Work. And since,
during the teen age, change is so rapid, I tried to check on it
once a month. It'll take me two chapters to spell it out for
you, but I think it'll be worth your time.

My object wasn't perfection. Not me. I'm a realist! It was
growth in all departments. But I actually took a pencil, listed
my aims under each heading, checked my progress, added
or revised the goals. (I found I had to revise downward sometimes, particularly in the financial area.)

Remember, this is strictly a do-it-yourself program. So

you might as well be honest from the start. It's what you think your potential is. You set the goals because you have to do the work. Your aims wouldn't be my aims, or even your parents' aims for you. You're different from anyone else in the world. God never made two hairs on anyone's head alike, or two talents, or two personalities, or two faces. Your potential is God-given. Unique! Wonderful! Your goal is to make the most of it in every way.

Pilgrim's Progress

FIRST: *Spiritual.* The road map for the adventure of your own Pilgrim's Progress should come from the Bible. This is my road map. I've already told you that I am a member of the Church of Christ. I believe it is the best, truest—the only.

Jack Spina, Randy Wood, Mort Lindsey and other members of our team are active members in other religious groups. We all believe in God and are sincerely trying to do His will. You should study your own Bible to find God's will for you. In this land of freedom each of us can find his way by applying himself to studying the record personally.

The point is, we need help. Exciting as the road is, it is no easy road. And so I recommend with all my soul, that every teen-ager seek the guidance offered by God's Word. If neither of your parents is a member of the church, you are old enough now to find the way yourself. If you are already serving God according to His directions in the Bible, it is time for you to renew the promises you once made. Part of your goal might be to refresh your understanding. To review your direction. To learn more about prayer. In other words, to grow along spiritual lines. To know God in a personal, intimate way.

My friend, please don't sell this short! Robert Louis Stevenson made a startling discovery at the age of four. "You can never be good," he observed to his mother, "unless you pray."

She asked him how he knew.

"Because," he replied, "I've tried it."

It is now time to make your own discoveries. I'd like to share some of mine with you in a later chapter. But make this portion of your check sheet carefully. Your whole future, your whole sense of identity, belonging, and purpose, may never become clear to you unless you start with your spiritual growth. Every other facet we discuss will actually hinge on what you believe. There really isn't any other way to begin a sound emotional growth, to learn to love where we have hated, to replace fear with confidence, erase doubt with faith.

Under this heading I personally wrote down certain Bible readings, a decision to give thanks before meals (even if I could only close my eyes for a second and say it silently), to ask for certain things and to pray for certain people, to have set times of prayer, and usually one commandment (to honor father and mother—to do unto others as I would have them do unto me—not to take God's name in vain) for special effort.

Don't think there isn't plenty of challenge here. The difficulty is not to be over-ambitious at first, not to bite off more than you can chew. Be realistic but faithful in a few things, until they become a grooved, automatic part of your consciousness. Then you can raise your sights and try to get the hang of a few more. The trick is to work at them.

Too many people think that a combination of God and prayer is going to do the whole job. Like the two little girls who were late for school. As they ran along, one little girl panted: "Let's stop and pray." The other had a better idea. "Let's keep running and pray as we run." We have to do our part!

P.S. Please don't be ashamed of these resolutions and good habits. Shirley and I ate dinner at Patti and Jerry Lewis' house the other night. I have seldom been more moved than

I was when Jerry expressed thanks, or "said grace," before we ate. You can imagine that his prayer was a little unorthodox—but very sincere. And if Jerry Lewis isn't embarrassed at giving thanks in front of friends, you and I needn't be, either.

The social animal

SECOND: <u>Social</u>. Let me say straight off that if you are in any confusion on whether to butter your crackers, or which way to spoon your soup, the authority is Emily Post. Not me.

What interested me when I made out my little list were basic rules for getting along smoothly in the world around me.

I found one thing pretty quick. I couldn't go far wrong on the purely social side if I honestly tried to practice the Golden Rule. Now, the Golden Rule is *not*, as one teenager wrote on his exam: "That the man who finds gold first keeps all of it." It is: "As ye would that men should do to you, do ye also to them." Or treat Joe the way you'd like him to treat you.

I'd say most good manners are just that one rule put into practice. We're not apt to slurp our soup in our neighbor's ear if we've considered how we'd feel if he returned the compliment.

So for my social check I simply put down the Golden Rule and checked against this one every night . . . in the beginning, much to my sorrow. But it helped me to improve my relationships with others. And it did make a surprising change in my manners.

In fact, it can be full of surprises. Like the man and woman who got on a bus, each having just heard of the Golden Rule. The man offered the woman his seat. She fainted. When she came to, she thanked him. He fainted.

I remember at various times putting questions on my list based on Christ's Sermon on the Mount. Did I ever "turn the other cheek" in a fight or an argument? Was I ever a peace-maker? At first my answers weren't very satisfactory compared to my aims, believe me! But they got better as I worked on 'em. That's the point. This is the surest way I know of to become easier to live with, to be a better friend, a more attractive person all round. And you begin to like yourself better, which is important! In fact, a lot of this world's troubles are caused by people who don't like themselves inside, and lash out at other people who seem better. I'd say that if we all concentrated on improving ourselves till we were the kind of people we ourselves like to know, the world would be better off.

But there is a second part to this social check that most of us teen-agers overlook because it is completely new to us. It is our responsibility to the world in which we live. Our duties as citizens and members of the community. Sounds pretty forbidding, doesn't it?

Well, it isn't. I found it can be fun. And if we're going along with the Jam Today theory, we can start right now. We can begin by doing the things our church suggests, definite things for our community, our nation, countries all round the world. We can become active in the student government of our school. We can take on the jobs of baby sitting, or driving older voters to the polls. We can read a good newspaper or news magazine and try to keep up with what's going on in the world nationally and internationally. Current events are something more than a torture dreamed up for school children. They're history in the making, that our children will be taking tests on! They form the world we'll be taking over, for we are what they say we are, the citizens of tomorrow. But, believe it or not, we are also citizens of today!

I know I ran for all kinds of offices at school, campaigned for my friends, voted on everything. Eventually I got elected to some offices, class prexy, student council, student body president in my senior year. But I'll tell you a secret. I didn't get it on my wavy hair, my white bucks, my voice, or by a gimmick. I had to work! Now, we can't all be elected. But we can all be active. And maybe you *will* be elected!

I'll tell you the <u>trick I found for starting</u>. *Take jobs other people don't want.* My first one was School Clean-Up Day. There wasn't any glory attached. Nobody else seemed to want to organize sweepers, mop-pushers, window washers. But I put it down on my social check list and did it. And that led to other things.

A ten-year-old friend of mine has just been appointed bathroom monitor at grammar school. Not very glamorous, maybe, but she's made a start. I'm betting she'll do a good job and end up as a class president some day.

Make this a definite, realistic, list of things you can do to be an active, contributing part of society. I believe this is a good tip.

Let's get wise to ourselves

THIRD: <u>*Mental*</u>. Our mental progress, naturally, includes our scholastic aims and goals. In my opinion these should be as high as we honestly think our potential will stand!

Do I hear groans? Don't leave me yet. When I still thought being grown-up would mean doing as I pleased I intended to adopt the hobo's slogan when I got to that dream state: "Here's to de Holiday! Bless de hull t'ree hundred and sixty-five of 'em!"

I approached my first day of school with the idea of getting it all over with as quickly as possible and getting back to the "Holiday." When I came home from the first grade, so the family story goes, and Mama asked what they'd taught me, I replied: "Not very much, I have to go again."

So I went. And I went. In fact I've just finished going this year. Because do you know what I came to believe about education? I think with most of us it's like a guy walking into a fancy restaurant and ordering a big dinner, everything from soup to nuts, paying for it, and then trying to sneak out without eating it.

It makes about that much sense to go to school and have this terrific feast, one we need, one we've paid for, all spread out before us—and then to get by with taking as little as possible, or to cut, or to play hookey, or fudge on exams, and think we're putting something over on the teachers. Does the waiter care if we eat that dinner?

Isn't that pretty silly, when you stop to think about it?

So far my experience has been that there isn't anything wrong with education. I should know. I've finished Burton Grammar School, David Lipscomb High School, a Bible centered school under the guidance of members of the Church of Christ, one year at David Lipscomb College, one year at North Texas State Teacher's College, and two years at Columbia University. There's more education around than ever before. That's one of the advantages our generation has. I suggest we leave the yelling about systems and methods of teaching to our elders and talk truth to each other.

Let's admit to ourselves that the guy or gal who wants an education can get one. There's some truth in the story of the boy whose father wanted to know why he was always at the bottom of the class. "It doesn't matter, Dad," said this young man. "We get the same instruction at both ends."

Is it the teachers' fault if we don't learn? Honestly?

Teaching is their job.

But learning is ours! We can take it or leave it.

Now, I am trusting you to understand straight talk. I'm sharing something with you that I feel very strongly about.

What is our attitude toward education? Do we deceive ourselves that we have all the answers, when we haven't even begun? That kind of thinking reminds me of a friend of mine, a very learned, elderly astronomer, who sat next to a high school girl at a Youth Banquet. She asked him what he did and he replied with honesty and humility, "I am a student of astonomy."

He told me that her eyes flew wide in surprise. "That's funny," she said. "I finished that last year."

I think myself that we need to get wise to what education is, why we need it, and then set our sights as high as the traffic will stand. Honesty and humility are fine approaches.

For me, this learning business has two parts.

First, acquiring knowledge and skills.

Let's get this straight. I'm no great cheer leader for a lot of education-just-for-education's sake. I don't discourage that, but most of us will have our hands full just learning the things we need to know to be happy and successful.

If you're a girl and know for certain that you want to be a home-maker, then tailor your pattern to fit that: First Aid (in case you get a son like me), Home Economics, the things you know you'll need, plus the things that you think will make your home a happier one.

If you're a fellow and you already know you want to be a machinist or a missionary, you can get plenty of guidance on how best to fit yourself for your particular life.

But remember that many of us change our minds. A lot of fellows who say they aren't even going to college because they want to be mechanics outgrow the hot-rod stage, decide to become lawyers, and, if they have set their high school educational sights too low, have to waste time catching up. Or a girl set on home-making doesn't acquire any job skills for the period before she marries . . . or brushes off college, maybe.

So, set your sights high, and list your interests and aims together with the grades you honestly think you can and should maintain.

Then get to work. I tried to find ways to avoid this. Maybe you have, too. I never did like homework much. Not in high school. Not in college. I used to try to take the curse off by studying while listening to Bob Hope, and copying down his jokes. Trouble was, when I tried to tell 'em his jokes fell flat, and I fell flat on the homework. The way I finally got it done was to apportion my time and then stick to the schedule. I'd figure so much time for each subject (including study periods)—and no telephoning, no copying jokes, no nothin' until it was done. I didn't always do this, but when I did, it worked!

The second part of learning is learning to think!

Don't laugh! Or decide you've been thinking all your life, because you might be surprised. I know I was.

This kind of thinking means taking your knowledge— facts, figures, civics lessons, history, current events—and sifting them through your mind until you reach a conclusion or an opinion of your own based on facts, knowledge, observation, or experience. It doesn't necessarily mean you'll come to agree with someone else. Me, for instance. It does mean you're beginning to have a considered reaction to what you learn. You are not a sheep following the flock any more.

New ideas and theories, new inventions, new concepts, new knowledge itself, come from thinkers. You might think about that for a while.

Until we can think, and do think, we are second-hand people. Echoes. Imitators, not using our own God-given intelligence and mental powers.

And as we acquire more knowledge, or more experience, or new facts, we will change these conclusions and ideas. This will keep us humble. Keep us from being overbearing about our new-found opinions. That is why my friend the astronomer truthfully said he was only "a student of astronomy.

A boy I knew who was fourteen, right in the middle of the in-between stage, once told me that the reason he was always in hot water was: "I want to be Daniel Boone and nobody will let me."

What he wanted was a frontier to conquer like my illustrious ancestor. And this boy figured because a lot of the territorial world had been discovered and civilized there were no more horizons. But he was wrong! The horizons challenging us today are limitless. There are still some unexplored areas around. Most of them, however, are in the mental and spiritual realm. They are open to the female of the species as much as to the male. But for such adventures we need a little more than Uncle Dan'l, more than an old flintlock, a dead eye, and a coonskin cap. *We need an education. And the ability to think.*

When you set down your goals in this mental area, remember the horizons and see if it won't help you raise your sights. Remember you don't have to wait until you have a long gray beard. Jam Today! Youth has amazing powers. They say you're never too old to do great things. Well, I say you're never too young, either.

Here's concrete, factual proof from history.

George Washington at seventeen got a certificate as a surveyor from William and Mary College; and at twenty-two won his first battle with the rank of Colonel.

Lafayette came to the American colonies at nineteen and at twenty was commissioned by Congress Major General in the Continental army.

Joan of Arc was sixteen when she raised the Siege of Orléans.

Edna St. Vincent Millay was fourteen when her first poem was published in a national magazine and twenty when her "Renascence" established her as one of America's leading poets.

Here's concrete, factual, proof from today:

At thirteen a youth in Salt Lake City became the youngest in the nation to hold an FCC license as a radio engineer. Last year, at nineteen, Paul Smith was a top disc-jockey in the same city.

Also last year, the only woman licensed by the Scripps Institute of Oceanography as a scientific skin diver was a seventeen-year-old pre-med student, Margot Hatcher of San Diego.

Three sixteen-year-olds amazed Convair technicians in 1956 by building their own rocket test stand in California, and a rocket with a ten-mile range that the technicians described as similar to the one they were working on.

It was a high school student who recently managed a feat which had stumped commercial chemists; Sandra Davis of Evanston, Illinois synthesized perfumes from organic material.

It was a fifteen-year-old girl, Sue Berkland, who founded and edited a Junior Journal which built a circulation of 40,000 teen-agers around the world.

We may not all do something so spectacular. We don't need to. There is something special, however, for each one of us. Four-H Clubs and Scouts do some wonderful, practical and artistic things individually and as a group. So do many others. But we never know what we can do until we try. (Did someone say that once before? Doesn't matter. It's true!)

Wouldn't you like to make the most of yourself? Why settle for less?

Give this one some real thought before you put it on your personal list. Be realistic. No moon shots yet! But don't sell yourself short, either!

Let me tell you a story that I really like:

It's about a little boy who was driving his dad crazy with questions like "Why does grass grow right side up?," while the older man was trying to read a magazine. His dad told him to ask his mother; he told him to go and play with his tinker toys. None of it worked. Finally the father had a bright idea. He tore a map of the world out of the magazine, then tore that map into pieces. He gave the pieces to Johnny and told him to put them back together. This, he figured, would take a good long while and he could read in peace.

Nothin' doin'. In two minutes flat the boy was back with the map perfectly put together. Since he had no knowledge of world geography, his dad was amazed. "How did you do it, Johnny?" he asked.

"Nothin' to it," said Johnny modestly. "There was a picture of a man on the other side. I just put the man together and the world came out right."

So you see what we are trying to do together. We are taking the pieces of you, your environment, your inheritance, your I.Q., your face, your figure, and seeing what you have to work with and how you want to put them together.

And that's about what this old world needs from each of us. If we put ourselves together right, the world's in better shape.

So now, none of these things can seem small or unimportant. Let's tackle the last three.

Fit as a fiddle

FOURTH: *Physical.* It always gave me a pain during the early teen years to have school teachers, lecturers, columnists, even parents, constantly reminding me to "wash-with-soap-every-day," to "brush-your-teeth-after-meals," to "put-on-clean-clothes," to "eat-three-meals-a-day" (try and stop me!), to sleep, exercise, stand up straight and the rest. They even felt we needed to be told how to breathe. ("From-the-diaphragm"!)

It doesn't make sense to me yet that we *need* these reminders. Why would boys who are going to have to depend on their health as part of their equipment for making a living —and mowing their lawns besides—break the normal laws of physical fitness? Yet athletic coaches tell me that many of them take better care of their cars than of their bodies!

It doesn't make sense to me that girls who want to be as pretty as possible, who intend to be feeding and caring for a whole family day after tomorrow, don't know how to feed and care for themselves today. Yet magazine articles, dietitians, beauticians, high school principals, all sigh over the high percentage of poor physical care and poor nutrition among teen-agers, even in top economic areas.

I'll have to take their word for it. And if you are not one of them, forgive me for this detailed list. I always had physical fitness on mine. But there were a good many of these I could eliminate because they'd been drummed into me so thoroughly I could as soon forget to breathe. ("From-the-diaphragm"!)

Here, for a check list, are the major departments in health for which we, as teen-agers on our new do-it-yourself plan, are now responsible:

(a) *Proper diet:* The primary rule here is—three balanced meals a day *starting with breakfast!* It is hard for me to believe that anyone has to be coaxed. Unless, of course, I am served squash, eggplant or oysters. Anything else, I can eat for breakfast, but not those three gems!

I like to eat. So do most teen-agers. The catch is that three meals doesn't simply mean stuffing ourselves at stated intervals. The experts throw in that word *balanced.* That means we have to get certain kinds of food daily for present health and energy plus prevention of things like tooth decay. (How do *you* feel about having a lot of unnecessary fillings?)

A good friend of mine who is a first rate dietitian heading a department in a big city says you can't claim to be properly nourished just because you tip the scales at a round figure. To illustrate she quotes:

> There was a young lady from Munich,
> Whose appetite simple was unich,
> "There's nothing like food,"
> She contentedly cooed,
> As she let out three tucks on her tunich.

"A case," points out my friend, "of being over fed and under nourished. Because you don't get over weight from eating a *lot* nearly so quickly as from eating the *wrong things* —like popcorn, sweets, and carbonated drinks. A 'unich' appetite for a lady—but not for a teen-ager."

Teen-age weight varies considerably. I always thought I was too skinny. Some of my friends thought they were too plump. Fad dieting or super-stuffing is out of bounds unless your doctor recommends it. Usually nature herself corrects the condition *either way* if we stick to the proper daily balanced diet. That means those three meals should include vegetables (yellow and green, cooked and raw), fruits (one citrus, one other), milk (three glasses), whole grain cereal or bread, meat or poultry, and eggs. Boy, I sound like those food charts! Still, what they say is true. So eat your squash!

Now, that isn't too tough! I learned this all at Mama's knee. And then I learned it again in school. I'll bet you did, too. But just for fun, check yourself on it for a couple of days.

(b) *Personal cleanliness:* This means a bath or shower daily (as if you didn't know) with soap, remembering that ears, neck, face, feet, and fingernails, are all attached to the human body. Personally I like a mild toilet water or perfume for girls and a shaving lotion for guys (after soap). I can remember that Daddy always smelled great after he'd showered and shaved and was ready for work.

When I was in the third grade a desire to imitate this fragrance got me pretty well mortified. I didn't know his exact magic but I found a bottle of pretty smelling stuff on Mama's bureau and sprinkled myself liberally. In our little reading circle at school the teacher kept sniffing. And sniffing. As we lined up for recess, me next to her, she gave one last sniff and looked right at me and said, surprised, "Oh, it's you!" I had to beat up three boys for calling me "Patricia"! It taught me the difference between perfume and shaving lotion. But remember. *After soap!* you have skin problems? More often than not, soap and good food will fix 'em.

(c) *Sleep:* Not less than eight hours per night for teen-agers. Better at nine or ten. (This I like.) More than ten and someone might call you L——zy. But less than eight, brother, what it can do to your disposition, looks, and vitality!

(d) *Exercise:* Just because we stop playing tag doesn't mean we're supposed to sit the rest of our life. As teen-agers we need to outline a possible program for ourselves based on our athletic interests and the facilities available, and *keep at it.* Don't give up that bicycle too soon. I rode mine all through high school, and my wife's when I was at college in Texas. With a full work-study-home load it was more than transportation. It was my daily exercise. And f'r goodness sakes, watch your posture. I know I sound like Aunt Clara but I can't help it. I promised to level with you and sometimes teen-agers look as if those extra inches were just too heavy to hold up, either standing or sitting.

(e) *Teeth:* All together now . . . "brush-teeth-after-each-meal-and-see-your-dentist-twice-a-year."

(f) *Hair:* Shampoo once a week. Brush for girls (Shirley says fifty strokes for cleanliness and shine!), massage for boys (let's keep it with us as long as we can!).

I always used to hate to wash my hair because I looked like a wind-swept haystack afterward. Then Mama recommended letting it dry under a stocking cap. Oh, boy—I looked like a painted egg. The answer was to let the barber cut it properly and *keep it cut.* I definitely recommend haircuts and washings for boys on the grounds of health and cleanliness, if nothing else.

(g) *Clean clothes:* Always and often. But Great Coogamooga! I didn't need to tell you that. I will tell you this, though. A famous tap dancer I know auditioned girls for a

tour. There were lots of applicants, all top-notch. He finally
picked one young lady who had appeared each time in the
same outfit. "It wasn't because that meant she needed the
job," he told me. "I knew a lot of them needed the job. It
was because every single day for four days her dress and little
white coat had been freshly washed, starched, and ironed.
Her personal freshness was attractive. But it told me a lot
about her character, too."

There may be extras you will want to add to this physical
fitness list if you have all these basic rules down to where
they are second nature. Do you know all you need to know
about care of the eyes, proper lights for study, reading, TV?
If not, do a little research. Do you know first aid? Would
you like to? Do you know the rules and precautions for air
raids? If not, you could appoint yourself the committee of
one in your home. It's physical care . . . and also a service
to society . . . a social service.

Whistle while you work

FIFTH: *Work.* You know, I almost committed a big breach
of faith with you on this area in our check list. I almost called
it "Creativity and Accomplishments" to sugar coat the pill.
Sho 'nuff! That's because the word "work" makes most of us
think of "Sixteen Tons, and What D'ya Get?" I was going
to slip it to you gently and never mention *work.*

But *work* is the word for it. That's the word I used in my
check list and it served the purpose. We are going to go into
it from a lot of angles later on and see if we can't help find
that real hidden talent of yours. We're going to find out that
work can be fun. Meanwhile, put it on your list now. And
then see later, if your ideas and mine, your aims and mine
are anything alike.

I'll tip you off to one thing. If you're in the "Yakkity-yak,
don't talk back, walk-yourself-to-the-laundermat, bring-in-

the-dog-and-put-out-the-cat" stage, you just haven't accepted reality. Because chores we have always with us. I know! I was there. Remember Rosemary? I haven't got rid of them yet, either, even if Rosemary is retired. The point is, if you get there first and *do* them, there won't be any "yakkity-yak."

Set down the things you think should come here. The work *you* see right *now* for you to do. And then when we come round to the chapter on talents—on Creativity and Accomplishments—let's see how they stack up with the ideas that unfolded to me from using this chart over some years of teen-age growing.

Brother, can you spare a dime?

SIXTH. *Financial.* Somehow, finances and work go together in the natural scheme of living. Actually work and money are the freedom twins. Money in the bank means greater freedom of mind and action and we don't get financial security without working for it (even the ones who inherit it have to work to keep it, to spend it wisely, to keep from wasting it.)

If we have the opposite of financial security, we usually have debt. Debt is a form of slavery, whether you're manacled to a finance company on the installment plan or beholden to some friend who has made you a loan.

Right now is the time to start developing sound financial practices. When you are old enough to work, you are old enough to save, to begin to pay your way in some things, to plan ahead. And if you make any headway with those spiritual values we talked about in the beginning, you will know you are old enough to *give,* to *share,* and to *contribute.*

We'll be going into this in more detail, but put it down on your list now, with the goals and aims you think are practical and possible for you right at this moment.

The sum total is YOU!

Remember, if we're agreed that this "maturity" is the kind of grown-up-ness we want, we have to grow along all these lines till we are fulfilling our potential. A potential is that which is *possible,* but not yet *actual.* You are a potential cook as long as there's just the possibility that you could learn. When you have learned, why then you have fulfilled your potential. Boom! You can cook!

Setting up this check list could be your first honest effort toward self-discipline (the kind that takes all the others off your back), which will be your first honest step toward maturity. You are holding a mirror up to your life. The sum total of where you now stand in all these areas is YOU as you are now; the sum total of your goals and aims is YOU as you *wish to be;* and the first time you sit down and check your progress you will discover whether or not you are an idle dreamer. Tell you what. I'm all for dreams as you'll see. But not for idle dreaming alone. I think you have to back your dreams with effort.

When you finish this chart you'll see how *you* rate *you!* You are putting together the man or woman you want to be.

4

April Love

Growing up is not all work and no play!

Just in case you have the mistaken notion that I was a boy saint or a hot-house plant, allow me to disclose another secret from my past. One of the first games I learned after I put away my sling shot was spin-the-bottle. We played it at an eighth grade party at a classmate's house. I was thirteen and so was the girl.

Her name was Wanda and when we left the circle I don't mind admitting I was scared to death. Finally I got up enough nerve to give her a peck on the cheek and she shrieked, "Pat Boone, you kiss like a cow!"

Experience speaking to innocence? Or did she know Rosemary?

Whichever, that first kiss was evidence of another teen-age symptom—a shy, awkward, longing to sing romantic duets with the opposite sex instead of masculine solos in the barn.

Parents are apt to take a dim view of these early symptoms, to try to clamp down on "such silliness." Grandparents, more tolerant, call it "puppy love." A doctor views it as "part of adolescence." But to us it's April Love . . . and it's new and exciting!

The teen age is the real springtime of Romance, with a

capital "R"—as fragile, gay, lovely, as apple blossoms. Does that sound corny? Well, people make songs about it—and we sing 'em. Maybe you'd be embarrassed to say it aloud, but I'm not. You see, I'm looking back on it, and I know what it is—or should be.

I know it isn't very substantial. That it bears about as much resemblance to mature love as apple blossoms to ripe apples. But that doesn't make it any less wonderful. Just as blossom time comes once a year, and is brief, so April love comes once in a lifetime and its season is very short—and very special.

It's a pretty delicate affair, this stepping into the boy-meets-girl role, and it can't stand too much pressure. It already has those villains of restlessness, inconsistency, indecision, and insecurity, to deal with. If we don't watch our play carefully, we have less chance of Jam Today and sound fruit tomorrow.

That's why there are definite rules to guide us during this time.

We can have all its gaiety, all its freshness, all its fun, our share of horrible yet delightful heartaches; do our experimenting without a third degree burn, *so long as we keep to the basic rules.*

Who made the rules? Probably every man and woman since Adam and Eve has had a hand in it.

It's like the father who said to his daughter: "Your young man stayed pretty late last night. Hasn't your mother spoken to you about this?"

And his daughter replied sweetly, "Yes, Mother says men haven't changed a bit."

The rules were made by people like this mother because truly, April Love doesn't change. It wears new clothes. It rides in a hot-rod instead of a horse-and-buggy. But somewhere, sometime, every boy and girl (your mother and father included) goes through the lovely agony of that first kiss.

Rules for a beginner

We already know the first rule. It's Jam Today. Don't rush! Enjoy what is appropriate to this moment. Remember, it won't ever come again.

How old should you be when you begin dating? That depends. I was thirteen. If you're well advanced physically and mentally (ahead of yourself in school) this may sort of force your social growth ahead a little. On the other hand, if you're thirteen and not yet interested or interesting, don't stew. You aren't backward or slow. You'll ease into it at the right time for *you*.

This first stage calls for mild forms of dating, mostly in groups. There are a lot of restrictions. Early hours, transportation by parents, short finances, and chaperons. Ugh!

If we'll admit to ourselves that, in the beginning, this is all pretty much a more grown-up game we're playing, it is easier to accept the rules. It's a new kind of hide-and-seek, a new form of tag in party dress. Isn't that so? Honest, now? Even if we play at going steady, and this really is too young to do more than play at it, it's just a new version of prisoner's base. We don't pin the tail on the donkey for a yo-yo. We spin a bottle for a kiss. But all games have rules and we might as well accept that.

Take the chaperon. A little dodging, a little griping, is permitted. It's part of the game, like griping at the umpire at the ball park. But if the umpire isn't there, it isn't a legitimate ball game. And if a thirteen-year-old-party doesn't have chaperons, either someone doesn't know the rules, or isn't playing by them. It isn't legit, and it's a good game to stay out of.

Activities at this early stage generally include "the early show" or a matinee, home parties, school and church activities, usually in a crowd, usually delivered and fetched by parents.

When I'm asked (and I *am* asked, much to my surprise) about my views on make-up for twelve, thirteen, and fourteen year olds, high heels, late hours, parties with the lights off, types of parties in general, I find myself feeling now, as a young parent, pretty much the way I felt when I was that age. I'm for the Middle of the Road, or Moderate Course. I kinda agree with the man of God who was approached by a lady on the subject of using rouge. "Well," he said, "some pious men object to it; others see no harm in it; I will hold to the middle course and allow you to wear it on one cheek."

Take kissing. Now, I believe that kissing is here to stay and I'm glad of it! I understand that the inhabitants of the Lapland Alps rub noses; the Andaman Islanders say "I love you" by blowing into one another's hands with a cooing murmur; the Fuegians pat and slap in affection. But we kiss. Starting in the early teens. Not that it should, but it does. I know. I was there. Now that I'm the father of four little girls I could wish that there were less kissing and more scrabble and parchesi. Do you know why?

Not for the usual negative reasons, although I go along with those. We all know that indiscriminate kissing, dancing in the dark, hanging around in cars, late dates at this early stage can lead to trouble. And that you miss a lot of fun with the nicer play-by-the-rules crowd. There is absolutely no need to rush clumsily into things that will have such beautiful meaning later on.

But I recommend the moderate course for another very positive reason. Kissing is not a game. Believe me! It means a lot more than just a pleasant pastime, a forfeit, or a test of popularity. I can tell you for sure that if you get to thinking of it that way, you're dead wrong. A kiss is a beautiful expression of love—real love. Not only that, it is a powerful stimulus of emotion. Kissing for fun is like playing with a beautiful candle in a roomful of dynamite! And it's like any other beautiful thing—when it ceases to be rare, it loses its value and much of its beauty. I really think it's better to amuse ourselves in some other way. For your own future enjoyment I say go bowling, or to a basketball game, or watch a good TV program (like the Pat Boone Chevy show!), at least for a while.

Take it easy. Keep to the middle course. No extremes.

Two clues to being attractive

These "popularity twins" hold true throughout all life. But they're especially important in the stage of budding romance.

Be kind! Be friendly!

Maybe I'm sensitive on these points because of that blamed cow. Remember, we're all touchy here and there in this new social romp. You can be the prettiest, the smartest, and still the most left out if you make other guys and gals feel uncomfortable at this stage. It can boomerang too, because the shy, awkward cluck at whose expense you make jokes today may turn into something pretty terrific next year. Even more important, it'll throw you 'way off on your spiritual and social check list (see Chapter 3).

Kindness does not mean violating your own principles because someone else wants you to. Never! It means, again, remembering the Golden Rule. It means remembering that, what with all those teen-age symptoms churning in us, and our feelings very close to the surface, the most attractive ones are those who can put the greatest number at their ease.

I remember one girl, Trudy, in our class, who was quite chunky, freckled, and wore spectacles. Maybe these things were against her but no one seemed to know it. She had the nicest disposition, always kind, always cheerful, and she always got asked to every party because it was pleasanter for all of us if Trudy was there.

Trudy had a great gift. She could listen. She could listen even if it hurt!

That brings me to a couple of don'ts. *Don't* try to be the life of the party. If you do something well, like playing the piano, you don't need to be coy. If you are asked, go ahead without coaxing. If you are not asked, don't try to attract attention, to star, to be a comedian. Be willing to be the audience for someone else. They'll just love you for it.

And *don't,* in your early enthusiasm for April Love, overlook the chance of forming *friendships* with the opposite sex. Some of these last a lot longer than the skyrocket romance.

These are the best rules I know for a starter. Take the Middle Course. Stay with your age group. Don't rush. Play by the local ground rules without too much protest. That way, you won't foul out. Above all, *be friendly, be kind* . . . and have fun!

To go, or not to go steady?

I went steady twice before I met Shirley. The first time I was a freshman in high school and almost fifteen. That lasted three weeks. The second time I was a sophomore. That lasted six months.

Once again I find myself straddling that Middle Course. In my experience there are reasons *for* and *against* going steady. I'll give the evidence and you be the jury.

One of the chief reasons I see *for* going steady is that it eliminates dating-just-for-the-sake-of-dating. I'm agin' that myself. It doesn't mean a thing really and usually just indicates an overdose of restlessness, insecurity, indecision, and inconsistency. I'm not callin' anyone names just for dating different people. Only the ones who date just to date, the I-don't-care-where-I'm-going, or-who-I'm-going-with, but-I'm-on-my-way kids, seem to be trying to prove something to somebody, maybe themselves.

I guess I was lucky. I always had so much else to do that "just dating" seemed a waste of time.

But if I was really interested in a girl I'd want to see her often and this leads very easily to the steady pattern. It does help to keep you from just rushing around.

Then, too, simply because you've lived through the planned-party stage doesn't mean you're now a complete social success. In state two you are a lot more on your own and that has its terrors. I wasn't backward or shy, but leave me with a strange girl and I couldn't think of a thing to talk about. Boy, it was torture!

Here you are, just introduced to someone who can make your heart flutter and you don't know a thing about each other. You don't know her interests, her rules, and she doesn't know yours. You don't know her family or what your reception will be if you call. I was always terrified by a jingle I saw:

> He went out one lovely night
>   To call upon a miss,
> And when he reached her residence
>   this.
>   like
>   stairs
>   up
>   ran
> He

> Her papa met him at the door,
>   He didn't see the miss,
> He'll not go there again though—
>   for
> He
>   went
>   down
>   stairs
>   like
>   this.

On the other hand, after a lot of effort, you get to know her. You not only like her a lot (all right, you *love* her, in

the best April sense) but you feel at ease with her. Her
mother feeds you cookies. Her father welcomes you at the
door. Your teen-age symptoms simmer down. You know
where you are and what's what.

So you go steady. You can see the advantages.

There's another thing a lot of parents overlook. We not
only need to feel secure at this age. We need to feel needed,
and wanted. We need to be special to someone. We need to
feel attractive and desirable, and an ideal steady meets these
needs.

Now, after these rosy reasons, what have I got against it?

Well, most parents think it means getting too serious. I'll
admit that going steady has to be serious or it isn't any fun. I
haven't forgotten that. But the danger is in being more than
April serious, and rushing into the behavior patterns of a
much later stage. If you skip over to September or October,
it's a cinch you won't enjoy your springtime to the full. And
that's sad.

Another thing is that it really asks too much of a sacrifice
at fifteen or sixteen. You not only sacrifice knowing other
likely dates, but the real tug in my case was being cut off from
my buddies. (I wouldn't know how girls feel about that.)
Going steady breeds possessiveness, and that's too bad. We
figure, at that age, that if we let the boy or girl out of our
sight, the spell is broken. Well, listen to Uncle Pat. 'Tain't
true!

The truth is, the more time you spend together the sooner
it's over. I think that's one valid beef older folks have; that
too often going steady involves a kind of strangle-hold slavery that plays the dickens with other departments of your
life. After all, you are just going steady in regard to romance.
You're not eliminating every male friend, every hobby,
chores, school interests, the all-round growth in your life.

*So I would say it's a wise guy and gal who are willing to
let there be some spaces in their togetherness.*

Charles Eugene (Pat) Boone.

Home to Leonia, New Jersey.

DON LOYD

Dining out with Shirley.

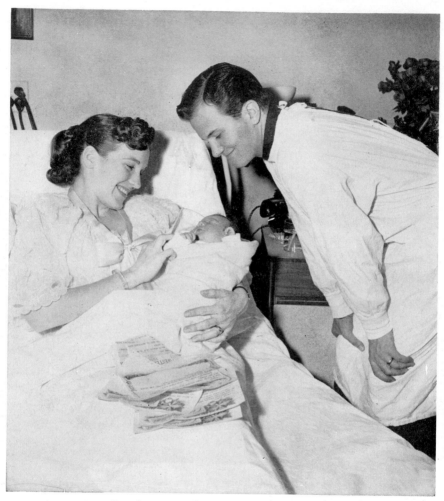

Getting acquainted with Laura Gene.

The four little Boones: Laura Gene in her mother's arms; then (*top to bottom*) Cheryl Lynn, Linda Lee, Debora Ann.

After Sunday Services at the Church of Christ, Beverly Hills, California.

GARY WAGNER

At the circus.

With a young friend.

GARY WAGNER

"I'll be home right away."

I think it's probably better if we don't go steady too soon. If, on the other hand, we feel we need to, then play by the April rules and don't try to force a full grown apple or an autumn leaf. Be satisfied with Jam Today.

Sweet sixteen

At fifteen and sixteen the rules have changed. We're not entirely free by a long shot. We still have to ask permissions. We haven't solved the finances completely. But we can stay out later, we can date without chaperons, transportation is easier. From the time I was sixteen I wanted a car the very worst way. Some of my pals had Model A's and T's. But my family wouldn't okay it till I was a senior and then I was never able to scrape together enough money. But I was allowed the family car on special dates, or I could double date with a friend who had one.

Now we have a lot of the same activities on a wider screen. The show, parties, bowling, sports events, church and school activities. We don't have to spin a bottle to get a kiss. On the other hand, there are even more rules of conduct for girls at this stage. One of them is that, even if a fellow runs like a three-legged hippopotamus, he must be the pursuer. In this game of hide-and-seek the male is always "it." The girl who makes the advance tips her hand immediately. That throws the game, for if she's "it" then the fellow has to run hide, and usually does. This I know, from experience.

Of course girls do have subtle ways of reversing the game. For example:

> There once was a maiden of Siam,
> Who said to her lover, young Kiam,
> "If you kiss me, of course
> You will have to use force—
> But you're certainly stronger than I am."

Undoubtedly, she got kissed. But down Nashville way, we would have seen through her. We didn't cotton to "bold" girls in Tennessee. The fact is that one of the best ways for a gal to catch a guy is let *him* chase *her!*

Then you came to the rules for "breaking up," and here's a fine game of Last Tag. Some fun. In the teens each party wants to say "I got you last." Nobody wants to be jilted, but nobody wants to be wrong, so the trick requires that you do the breaking up, but that it was the other's fault. Get it? (Since this game cannot be played except in twos, this makes for confusion.) And woe to the male who doesn't carry his torch like a gentleman. There can be real hard feelings if you play it wrong, like Mary, a teen-ager, whose mother had heard that she and Bill weren't going steady any more.

"That's right," Mary wailed. "And Bill behaved terribly."

"But I thought you broke it up," her mother said, surprised.

"I did," sighed Mary, "but Bill made absolutely no fuss about it."

Oh, those teen-age torches! Half real hurting pain, half the drama of a roman candle on the Fourth of July. I've always enjoyed being happy. It's part of my creed. So I never hung on to pain. But I've watched friends eat their hearts out in small bites and enjoy every tortured minute of it. Don't get me wrong—I know the pain is real, very real. But you must admit that it heals pretty quick if we let it.

The rules for being attractive become a little deeper at sweet sixteen. More is expected of you. You have to be friendly and kind *plus*. . . .

Take my first steady. The one that broke up in three weeks. She was a very pretty girl, a wonderful singer, much in demand. But she put too much strain on young love. She let me see her in her curlers. Invited me over when she was suffering from a cold in the head. Next thing you know, even when she was all fixed up I could still see those curlers and that runny nose.

Sad, isn't it? But that's the teen-age male. No matter what the other girls tell you, I say, *if you want to be attractive to boys always look your best!* Let the other gals wear Dad's shirts and sloppy blue jeans—you'll have the guys all to your-self.

There's a tip, too, in what broke up my second round of going steady. This girl was older than I, and that was all right for a while. But after six months things just cooled off and died. The reason? We didn't have very much in com-mon. She had moved on into a semi-summer league and I still happily belonged with the apple blossom kids. The teen-age temptation is to fall for someone's eyelashes, or a pretty fig-ger. But you can't really enjoy a romance unless you have some interests in common—church, school activities, friends, aims, ambitions, *something.*

Take it from me, *the girl who will attract the most worth-while guy and hold onto him longest, and vice versa, will be the one who is farthest along on that all-round road to ma-turity. Maturity—being useful, happy, well adjusted people with varied interests, able to give as much as we get—begins really to pay off in charm at this point where you're pushing from April into May.*

The part that lasts longest

The chief gift most people remember from April love is wonderful memories. And those we should have. But that's only half the story. If you think I've been treating it lightly, you're mistaken. Gaily, yes. Because gay it is. Lightly, never! It's too important.

For, you see, while it is true that the romances of the teens rarely last till summer comes, their influence can last a whole lifetime. I am thinking in particular of what happened to a famous athlete I always admired.

Bob Richards, Olympic pole-vault star, tells how he ran

with a teen-age gang in his home town that was tougher than most. They fought, swore, stole fruit. He never stopped to think where this behavior might lead.

Then he tried to date a girl he much admired in high school and she told him frankly that she "only went out with Christian boys." Astounded, Bob recalled that he had not thought of going to church for ten years. This nagged and nagged at him until one Sunday morning, without waiting to put on his socks or tie, he dashed to church.

Five of the fellows in that crowd later went to jail for holding up a gas station. Bob never got that date. But the girl gave him something better. For Bob Richards became an Olympic athlete, a religious leader, and a popular and respected citizen of the world. A true story, friend!

What might have happened, do you think, if those other five guys had met and admired real Christian girls? What would have happened to Bob Richards if *you* had been the girl he tried to date?

It's right to treat our young loves gaily. To enjoy them. But it's wrong to overlook their mighty influence in these vital years. We have a certain responsibility to everyone who honors us with their admiration. We can't possibly walk through life with each one. But something of us will go with them forever.

What would we like to leave in their lives? What would we like to give to each other from our early love to be remembered and possibly cherished for as long as we both shall live?

The answer is up to us!

5

The Happy Home Corporation

Once, at one of our eighth grade parties, a Ouija board predicted that I would have eleven children and play center field for the New York Yankees. So far Mickey Mantle still looks safe in Yankee Stadium, but Shirley and I have a fair start on the family.

To date we've celebrated five anniversaries and four stork calls. And I'd say one of the big thrills of being grown up is to be co-founder of a happy home.

Is there any way to guarantee, despite all that we see and hear, that a home can be happy? I firmly believe there is. Not a home without trials, without growing pains. Not that Cloud Nine pipe dream where everyone can "do as I please." But if both parties are willing to make the effort, my experience is that April love can ripen into the mature love that is the corner stone of a genuinely warm, satisfying, home life.

Courtship—April to May

I met Shirley just before Christmas in our junior year at high school. She transferred to David Lipscomb to live in the dormitory while her mother underwent surgery. Her reputation as a real knockout and the singing daughter of TV's singing star, Red Foley, gave her a great build up. Shirley, in person, was no letdown!

We met the day of a tremendous snowstorm that conveniently closed school for several days. At the end of those days of dating on sleds, skimming down hills, crashing through bushes, walking over a mile through a Christmas card landscape to my house, I think it was the way I began to feel about Shirley that brought on the thaw.

From then on we saw each other steadily and had all the fun and gaiety of an April romance. Then, in our senior year we exchanged school rings. Shortly after that, the death of Shirley's mother brought us very close together. The honest sharing of a deep grief can bring a new mature quality to romance. At this point we moved on into May and began to talk seriously of marriage.

For the first time I thought of a girl not as a "steady" but as a possible wife. Not merely as someone to kiss under a full moon but to love and cherish even with a runny nose. I don't think this moment comes until we are really ready for it. I know it shouldn't come until we really meet the One-And-Only who fulfills all the dreams we've built up during our early experiments.

Why was I so sure Shirley was and is the OAO for me?

First: She has the kind of beauty I admire. A neatness, a freshness and cleanness, as well as pretty features. Her physical attractiveness is the quiet, decent kind that a man looks for in a wife. In a word, for me, she has personal charm.

Second: She has a great spirit of fun. For Shirley it is always Jam Today and things never bog down where she is. Her interests have always been varied—school activities, current events, studies, sports. She can beat me at ping-pong or swimming and still be completely feminine. *She is a good companion.*

Third: Personality-wise, Shirley has always been kind and friendly. She genuinely likes people, will go to great lengths to help them, has been swell to my friends. *She guides her social life by the Golden Rule.*

Fourth: I found, as we grew to know each other well, that Shirley is a woman of principle. She has a quiet strength (which, when I do not agree, I call stubbornness), and once she has made up her mind that a thing is wrong, nothing can move her. *She is the sort of woman you can trust with the things that matter most to you.*

Wouldn't you say that I am describing a girl who has approached the maturity we aimed at on our check list?

And what did Shirley see in me? Well, that's her secret. She used to say she liked my white buck shoes, my nonchalant air, my fast peg to first base, the whispery groans I tried to pass off as singing, and my thrice-broken nose. This I doubt.

I know I made her laugh by just being me, and that helped. But when I pin her down she says I am to tell you that she first began to think of me "seriously" when her mother died and she became convinced of the honesty of my religious beliefs. She says she also became convinced I could "always take care of a family even if it meant milking cows!", and, further, she believed I would finish what I started (and today only wishes either she had been wrong or that I wouldn't start so many things). I don't know whether her sense of fun is running away with her or whether she will change her mind tomorrow. But that's what she says tonight!

Well, so we were going May-steady in our senior year and talking about getting married. But we were sensible. Shirley was to start nurses' training when school was out and I had four years of college ahead. We would wait. And then two things happened that pushed us right on into June. Remember, I told you that the time will surely come when you can marry, earn a living. Well, for us that time had come.

Teen-age bride and groom

Shirley and I eloped in the beginning of my sophomore
year in college. We were both nineteen. While I wouldn't
change a minute of it, I don't recommend either elopement
or teen-age marriage and I'll tell you why.

But first let me tell you why we decided to elope.

Remember, we discussed how parents could think that
going steady could get too serious? Well, my parents became
converted to that view. They loved Shirley but they were
afraid we'd get married too soon and I'd give up the education for which I'd planned and saved so long. They asked us
to slow down, to stop seeing each other, and we sincerely
tried.

But it didn't have the desired effect. Dating someone
else, we both found, was a "pretend," a deceit to ourselves
and them. Pretty soon we were going places separately, hop-
ing to meet accidentally-on-purpose and I would take Shirley
home. Once I had an operation and even then felt I needed
to see my girl. So Shirley would sneak up the hospital stairs
after hours to visit me. Only neither of us found that very romantic. We felt sneaky. And that went against the grain.

Here was a crisis in principles. At our age, with only a left
hand and an eyelash remaining in the teens, was it worse to
do what we wished openly and frankly? Or be sly and deceit-
ful?

Now there's a problem. When are we old enough to take
our stand on what we think we must do even if it opposes our
parents' views? Right then I couldn't answer that one.

Then came the second blow. Shirley's father was planning
to pull up stakes and move to Springfield, Missouri. That
meant complete separation. We faced a crisis. We had to find
that answer.

It occurred to me that we are "old enough" to make our
own decisions when we are mature enough to face the conse-

quences; to see our responsibilities and discipline ourselves to fulfill them all.

Could I be married and finish college? Could I work, support Shirley, and still attend school? It seemed to me absolutely necessary, a point of honor, that if we made an independent decision to marry without family approval, we be able to prove ourselves independent of family help.

My check sheet, my past experience in "work" and "finances," led me to feel confident that, if it meant that much to me, I could do it. And what really meant the most to us? What were our lifetime aims? A family. A happy home. An education. No separation. No sneaking.

We hadn't rushed. We had given April and May their due. Now should we say goodbye to them? It meant the teen age was over and manhood at my front door after seven short years. I'll admit I was a little scared. But, as I've heard them say at Yankee Stadium, you don't get ahead without some risk. You can't steal second with your foot on first.

We were married in Springfield, Tennessee, on a beautiful Saturday afternoon in the fall of 1953.

Now, here's why I don't recommend elopements.

Mama told me, long before I knew Shirley: "I may oppose you when you want to get married. I might oppose you right up to the last minute. But when you do, that's that. We won't mention it again and I'll welcome your wife as my daughter."

I think most parents feel the same way. I told you I'd share my mistakes with you and here's one I made. To avoid being sneaky I did a big sneak. And while my parents, who really love Shirley and really welcomed her as my wife, were swell about it, they couldn't conceal their shock and disappointment and hurt. I wish now I'd had the courage of my convictions; come home and said quite openly what we planned to do. But I didn't. And Mama didn't even offer to spank me. It hurt that much.

Now here's why I wouldn't recommend teen-age marriage

unless your maturity check sheet is literally covered with gold stars (which mine was not). The chief wrangle in a young marriage, particularly if you want a family and haven't finished school, is a time-money problem. It is hard on the bridegroom's nerves and physical stamina and hard on the bride's tear ducts. For quite a while Jam Today seems a myth because you can never seem to catch up with today.

As newly-weds we took a small apartment near the college, furnished haphazardly out of family attics, and I got a job at a radio station. With me at the panel nights and holidays cutting us into the national network, putting on transcriptions and tapes, doing commercials, studying in between, it was amateur night every night on Station WSIX. I was there Christmas Eve and New Year's Day, and, what with classes in between, Shirley and I saw each other for lunch once in a while, late at night and very early in the morning.

It was a good thing my wife was the kind of girl she was, or we might have bogged down. A lot of young marriages fall apart because of this very thing. And more often, the joy and fun of adjusting to the husband-wife situation is over too soon because of the strain and responsibility of making a living under the tremendous handicaps of youth, inexperience, and divided interests.

There didn't seem to be any way to apportion the time because there simply wasn't enough of it (or money either after I took a flyer in chinchillas with our savings . . . but that happened in Texas). Anyhow, we seemed to get into time-debt and it seems we've never got completely free.

I cannot give you any rules for handling this difficulty except to avoid getting into it if possible, and if not, to make the best of it and pray!

In January we took our five month old marriage to Denton, Texas, because things "would be easier there." This is called the "geographic cure." It doesn't work.

Supposedly, with North Texas State Teacher's College at

Denton, the apex of a triangle including Ft. Worth and Dallas, two good radio and TV towns, there would be plenty of both work and education for me. NTSC has great speech and music departments, and I was interested in both. Friends of friends of ours lived in Denton and raised chinchillas (but I am not going into that because there's one mistake I am very tender about!) Things somehow would be "easier" for Shirley, and somehow all our problems would be solved.

Starting off for Denton was high adventure, all right. I had bought my first car—a green '53 Chevy sedan from Daddy shortly before our marriage. Now we piled all our worldly goods into a rented wagon and hauled for the wide open spaces. We were armed with excellent letters of recommendation. And supreme faith. (This commodity no marriage should be without!)

I might say here that Shirley's sense of fun was a lifesaver. While nothing ever completely solved the time-money problem but time and more money, we did hit on one rule that both of us think solves the basic friction that has to happen when two people, very much in love, but very young, have to begin to work as a team. It helped us, anyway—and so I'll pass it along.

We call it the "president-of-the-corporation" rule.

President of the corporation—family style

In the very early days of our marriage we had quite a few discussions and differences of opinion. They kept on and on because they were never really solved. Shirley thought marriage should be a fifty-fifty deal with first one, then the other, having the final say; only there were no rules about who would have it when, and we weren't polite about taking turns.

This is not unusual. It'll happen to you.

I had always felt that one person had to have the final say —and that that one had to be the husband. (Time out to re-

vive any girls who just fainted.) I know it sounds "old fash-
ioned," but I'm sharing my honest thoughts and experiences
with you, and I have reasons. I don't believe a girl will ever
truly respect a man who lets her walk all over him. The
reason is that then he isn't a man.

I'm not recommending a return to the caveman. And I
do believe that marriage is a fifty-fifty deal, but every corporation has to have a president who, when the chips are down,
can say, "It's going to be this way." If not, there's too much
confusion and indecision. And bitterness.

After we hit Texas and Shirley came around to trying this
scheme, she found we had more stability and that I was more
inclined to be generous and see her side if I knew the decision rested with me. I didn't have to fight for my manhood
any more. Naturally I like this arrangement because I am a
normal male. Shirley likes it because she is a normal female.
She wants me to take care of her and our family. All right,
she has to let me do it.

You'd be surprised how this works to her advantage. You
take the division of labor. I remember after the babies started
arriving (and they are all "why—y" babies, which proves
out in one letter in each of their nicknames, Cherry, Lindy,
Debby, Laury) and there were trips to the dentist or Debby
broke her nose, or the whole tribe had the mumps, or their
mother had to go shopping, this was all brought to the president of the corporation for solution. When the vice-president
in charge of housekeeping needed (or still needs) additional
help in the kitchen, changing diapers, hanging out wash,
baby sitting, etc., the president, as a good executive, has to
send somebody—and most of the time in Texas there wasn't
anybody to send but me.

Sometimes, girls, if you let your husband boss the project
a little, he'll wind up doing the work quite efficiently. Because, you see, it's *his* corporation.

It was in Texas, really, on a salary of $44.50 a week, with a newborn daughter, Cherry, that we finished our shake-down cruise and began to lay the foundation for a happy home. Don't misunderstand. We had a lot of fun from the start despite time-work-money-adjustment of personality difficulties. Because we were young and in love. But in a way, that was just playing another, much more grown-up, game under trying circumstances. It took us a while to begin to learn the rules for a steady, happy, married life. The first was the president-of-the-corporation rule.

Looking back, I find that my check sheet (which I still evaluated once in a while) now had some pretty stiff aims and goals, and also words of wisdom gleaned from various sources that seemed helpful to me in establishing a really fine husband-wife-family relationship.

I know these are mostly rules for a tomorrow that probably hasn't come to you. But there's a lot you can begin to practice now. The rest I'll pass along and maybe, when *the* time does come, you'll remember and they'll help you as they helped us:

MAXIMS ON MARRIAGE
As collected, with notes and comments
by
P. BOONE
(happy husband of one wife, proud father of four female offspring)
now humbly offered to teen-agers as Truths I've Tested.

1. *Don't expect perfection. If you do you're not ready for marriage yet awhile.*
   He: "How come you aren't married?"
   She: "I'm looking for the perfect man."
   He: "Haven't you found him?"
   She: "Yes, but he was looking for the perfect woman."
2. *Be willing to WORK at making your home a success.*

"The world is full of willing people—some willing to work, the rest willing to let them. (Robert Frost.) Where do I fit?

Some persons are like wheelbarrows. They stay still unless they are pushed. Self-starters make the best mates.

Marriages may be made in heaven but we are responsible for the maintenance work. Who, me? Yes, you!

3. *Girls—Learn the jobs necessary to your business—homemaking.* (Contributed by S. Boone.)

Her mother: "My daughter sings, plays the piano, paints, understands botany, zoology, French, Italian—in fact, is accomplished in every way. And you, sir?"

Prospective son-in-law: "Well, in an emergency, I suppose I could cook a little and mend socks."

4. *Apply the Golden Rule in your attitude and conversation around the house.*

Faith, hope, and charity, should *all* begin at home!

To believe in men is the first step in helping them. You can start with your husband or wife. Loyalty and faith generate power in marriage.

A retentive memory is a good thing—but the ability to forget is the true token of greatness (Elbert Hubbard). It is of no use to *forgive* if you can't *forget* (P. Boone).

Many a wife has made her own marital grave with a series of little digs. And vice versa. This can be observed by any alert citizen!

Often the difference between a successful marriage and a mediocre one consists of leaving about three or four things a day unsaid (Harland Miller). Unkind, mean, gossipy, things particularly.

5. *Learn to laugh at yourself . . . at your mistakes. Laughter releases tensions and puts things back in proper perspective.*

You grow up the day you have your first real laugh—at yourself (Ethel Barrymore).

6. *Found your home on faith, prayer, kindness, cheerfulness to make it a happy, magnetic center for family life.*

If we want better people to make a better world, then we will have to begin where people are made—in the family.

And good luck to you! Start today to be the happy home-makers of tomorrow.

Signed: Pat Boone, President
The Charles Eugene Boone Happy Home Corporation.

Endorsed by: The Board of Directors:
Shirley Foley Boone, executive vice-president
Cheryl Lynn Boone, first vice-president
Linda Lee Boone, second vice-president
Deborah Ann Boone, third vice-president
Laura Gene Boone, fourth vice-president

6

To Be a Friend

This morning I had a letter from a teen-age girl in Indianapolis. "My mother," she wrote, "is worried because I am not as popular as she was at my age. It makes me feel pretty low and I guess I try too hard, or don't try hard enough, or try the wrong way or something, because it is true that I am not the type that attracts friends."

You'd be surprised at how many letters like this I see each week. Teen-agers wanting to know—"How can I be more popular?" How can I make the girls like me? Or the boys? The old saying is that all the world loves a lover—but I believe that all the world wants and needs friendship.

Loneliness makes people suffer at any age, not just the teens, because they feel separate from the human race. And we all want to belong.

But I'd like to get one thing straight—fast! I don't think popularity and having friends are the same thing at all. Popularity—"manifest approval of the people in general"—can be a good, sound thing, but it can also be a personality freak or a snow job. Adolf Hitler was the most popular man in Germany for quite a spell.

I'd say we can be top dog in the popularity cult and be so busy trying to win the approval of people in general that we may not make trustworthy or honest or loyal friends at all. This isn't sour grapes. Both Shirley and I won popularity contests in high school. It was very nice but not permanent. What lasted were my friendships with guys like Don Henley (since grammar school) and Billy Potter (since high school), and Mack Craig, my high school principal.

So my advice would be to learn the art of friendship first. Then, if general popularity follows, well and good. If it doesn't, you'll never miss it, because you'll be busy with your friends.

What made me feel sorry for this girl who wrote me was not what her mother thought (although this can be hard to take, as we'll discuss in the next chapter), but the fact that she says she is "not the type that attracts friends."

All of us can and should be that type. There isn't any need for us to be lonely, truly there isn't. She surely must be trying too hard, or not trying hard enough, or trying in the wrong way, because all you have to do to have friends is *be* a friend. Now I didn't dream that up. That isn't original with me any more than the Golden Rule. It's an all time truth! Even if we aren't lonely most of us have a lot to learn about the art of being a real pal.

One father pointed this out to his daughter in a pretty neat way. The girl came home one evening and her Dad asked if it had been a nice party.

"Oh, yes," she said, "I enjoyed myself very much."

"That isn't what I asked," her father said. "Did everybody enjoy himself? And what did you contribute?"

He was encouraging her to be a better friend, to think more of others and less of herself.

Just what does it take to be a friend? Do we have it? Let's

try an inventory, the good along with the bad, and find out. I'll take mine and you can try it on for size yourself.

What kind of a friend am I?

Am I sincere? That I am. When I like a guy or a gal I really like 'em. I'm not collecting smiles to make me feel good or win a popularity poll. I like people. I really do. And that's a big help in starting a friendship. Oh, now and then I'm friendly with a guy I don't particularly cherish—everybody has to be now and then. But on the whole I try to be very sincere in my dealings with folks.

Am I honest? I try to be, but I'm not always as tactful as I should be. I've always felt that a valuable friend will cut you off at the knee, if you start goofing. (My pal, Don Henley, sure gets a gold star here.) But to keep us from being "reformers" or old maids or picking on each other, I guess we should balance that with honest cheers when a friend does something nice or right. You agree? It isn't fair to pick on a guy's faults and take his virtues for granted.

Am I loyal? Definitely, almost to a fault, and that is possible. As teen-agers we develop such feverish loyalties to one another that adults have a hard time understanding it. If our aims aren't high and our honesty between ourselves is a little thin, this can be dangerous. You know it! We can cover-up for a friend some trouble or mistake that might better be out in the open. But I'm all for real loyalty. In fact I think we should spread it around a little.

Here's a tip. If you are loyal to your family to begin with, and don't talk about their personal business outside your own home, you won't put a needless burden on friendship. I've known this betrayal of family troubles to be very embarrassing both ways.

Am I trustworthy? One of the things you like most in a teen-age friend is to know you can trust him with your confidences. I've made special efforts along these lines, and I'll admit it isn't always easy, or that I always succeeded. Friends fall out and we have to resist talking about them or betraying them even when our feelings are hurt or we're sore. We have also to resist the temptation to pass a confidence from one very good friend to another very good friend under an oath of secrecy. Remember, loyalty demands that we only confide what is our own business.

A technique for doing this was worked out by Col. Frank Knox when he was Secretary of the Navy. Some good friend thoughtlessly asked him about the movement of certain ships. Col. Knox leaned over very confidentially and asked, "Can you keep a secret?"

"Certainly," his friend responded.

"Well," grinned the Colonel, "so can I!"

Am I good company? This is largely a matter of disposition, cheerfulness, kindness, that old ability to put others at their ease and make them feel good. But, believe me, it's also a question of common courtesy and good manners.

Before we hit the teen age, the law of the jungle is apt to prevail. It is socially acceptable for one friend to hit another over the head with his tinker toys if things don't go his way. But by the time we reach the teens we've discovered that our relationships at parties, school, home, between each other, in little things as well as big ones, just won't stand this jungle-type friction. If we're the ones who create friction, we're squeaky wheels and not at all attractive.

Courtesy (and this includes consideration in such areas as use of the telephone, borrowing, please-and-thank-you, table manners)—*all* courtesy is simply the oil we use to keep the machinery of friendship running smoothly. Element'ry, Watson.

Am I consistently thoughtful and dependable? Since we're being honest with each other, my personal answer, in a word, is "no!" Take out the word "consistently" or add "in big things" and I might get by. But I very often mean to do

things, even promise to do them, and then get side-tracked. I
excuse myself by saying I'm busy, but it's only an excuse. I
could and should do better. This I don't like in other people and I sometimes wonder if I'd have myself for a friend.
Maybe not.

The kind of people I like and try to win for my personal
friends are those who take the time and trouble to express
what I only feel. I always hope some of it will rub off on me.
Let me tell you about Mack Craig. He is my idea of a real
friend.

Mack was principal at David Lipscomb High School while
I was there, and now is dean of the college, an exciting
teacher who was also studying for his Ph.D., taking care of his
own family, preaching at a church in White's Creek every
Sunday. He's usually about as skinny as my wrist, half because
he never takes time to eat, half because he's forever loping
along at a fast trot trying to keep everybody happy.

Whenever I was worried or had a decision to make I'd take
a walk with Mack, or call at his home, or even wake him
at some horrible hour in the morning. Because I trusted
him completely to be sincere, honest, loyal, to keep my confidence—all the things we've been questioning ourselves on
—he was the one I turned to with that big question of Shirley's and my elopement. Mack gave me what advice he could
and then said when we had decided honestly what we thought
was right, he'd stick by us. And he did.

Friendship has played a large part in my career, too. I was
lucky enough to meet Jack Spina and Randy Wood, my co-
managers, early in the game. We're in business together,
true, but both of them have taken the trouble to understand
my personal convictions and to help me stand by them pro-
fessionally even when it cost us money. Like the time we were
offered a chance to record a brand new rock-'n'-roll song. We
all thought it was going to be a sure hit, but the lyrics were

suggestive and so we didn't record it. Another singer did with changed lyrics, and it sold over a million records. Wish I'd thought of changing the lyrics! But you can see what it means to me to find friends in the business world who are willing to put sound principles ahead of material gain. That's something!

Because this thoughtful, dependable, friendship goes right down the line from Jack and Randy and Don Henley, to Len Gochman who took over as "right arm" when Uncle Sam tapped Don for the service, to Mort Lindsey, my accompanist and musical director on our TV show, to Dick Overstake, who manages our publishing company, and right down the line of our co-workers, we manage to function "family style." (I wish all families could be as happy!) This means, of course, a lot of laughs and clowning in our work, and hardly any friction.

Isn't that some way to run a business? We get it done, painlessly, harmoniously, successfully, and have fun doing it. Wouldn't that be a great way to run a home, or a school, or a club, or even a country? But the reason it's possible is that every one of us is willing to put the good of the whole ahead of his personal good. I really think each of our co-workers is more interested in what they can give than what they can get.

That's the *Secret of Cooga Mooga,* our corporation!

Everything we do in life, whether in business, or church, or school, at home, at a party, or just getting along with the guy next door is really an adventure in human relations. Just stop and think about that a minute. Isn't it true?

Well, if we put to work all these ingredients for friendship we've been talking about in our dealings with all people—older, younger, our age, male and female—if we can honestly, from the heart, begin to try to give instead of get, we'll come out happy, successful, properly popular folk. In fact, you could say that the surest way to receive is to give. It really works.

We can't fail! This is the law of attraction.

What have I got to give?

In another letter that came in the morning mail a young guy complains that he isn't well liked because "I don't excel at anything and I can't keep up with the rest because my dad's been out of a job and we need every penny at home."

I don't think that's an honest reason for crawling into your shell and giving up. I've already told you that we didn't have a lot of material things and few of my friends played star quarter-back or ran a four minute mile, either.

Look at it this way. You have a dollar and I have a dollar. We're friends. Well, I give my dollar to you and you give your dollar to me. Nobody is any richer. That's just an exchange.

But supposing I have a problem or burden and you have one. We're friends. I share mine with you and your understanding makes my heart easier. And the other way 'round. We've got it off our chests. Actually, in the act of sharing our problem each one of us has lightened his load.

Now, you have a thought or a great idea and I have one. We're friends. I share mine with you and you share yours with me. Now we both have two ideas. We gained the least when we gave material things. We gave the most when we gave sympathy and ideas—in other words, when we gave of ourselves.

In this light doesn't everyone have something special to give?

I don't think the fellow who wrote to me is facing his problem squarely. He's blaming outside things over which he has no control for his own failure. Actually he has plenty to give, but he probably hasn't learned to give it. And so it is with a lot of us. It just doesn't come naturally with all persons—this ability to get themselves across.

We hear a lot about two kinds of people, the extrovert, or out-going type, and the introvert, or shy one. The extreme extrovert, during the teen age, is apt to be so overwhelming that he scares people off or embarrasses them. I shudder when I think of the young gate-crasher at a Hollywood party who clapped John Barrymore on the shoulder and said: "Hi, Barrymore, old boy!"

And the great Barrymore looked at him coldly and said, "Don't be formal. Call me kid."

This is the show-off, the palsy-walsy-loud-voiced-life-of-the-party enthusiast. He wants very much to give but he needs to tone down. This simply isn't the way to win friends or persuade anybody. There's a female of this species as well who simply attracts too much attention to herself in her eagerness to be noticed and liked. Unhappily it has the reverse effect.

On the other hand, the shyness of the extreme introvert is agony even to watch. A man who suffered from shyness right into adult life is Lawrence Welk, who tells the story on himself of being so nervous at a public appearance that he announced his Champagne Music Makers would give the audience some Shampoo Music. Yet Lawrence Welk says he lost all the suffering when he simply accepted his shyness as he accepted the color of his hair. He came to feel that it was no disgrace to be shy unless you were driven out of action by it. He even thinks that shy people have something special to give because they are usually very sensitive, very understanding and gentle, and truly sympathetic.

There isn't any sense in saying to these extremists "don't be so pushy" or "don't be so shy," because honestly, they don't do it on purpose. They want and need friends just as much as anyone does if not more (and if you personally don't happen to fall into either category you might be the one to help them overcome their problem; this might be your opportunity to be a friend; to give instead of get). But if you do find you are being rejected for either of these reasons, try to understand that everyone has something fine and special to give (including you) and that there is someone waiting to receive it. It's God-given, believe me, and so it doesn't need to be oversold by constantly drawing attention to it; or undersold by trying to hide it in a corner.

In either case, if you can relax and let Him open the doors, rely more on Him and less on yourself, you will find you are getting more attractive because your mind will be free to concentrate on the other fellow and his needs and less on how he is reacting to you.

It's a hard-to-take truth, but both the over-bold and the over-shy really suffer from being too self-centered. Not selfish. They may, in fact, be very generous. But just too occupied with "me and what people think of me." This knack of attracting friends requires just the opposite frame of mind. "I am thinking of *you*, and what I can do for *you*."

What have I got to say?

Conversation is the most useful form of communicating with others. I'm not denying that communication can be made with the eyes, a smile, a frown, or even a right to the jaw. But conversation is the most usual. It can be a great help to you in making friends or the exact opposite. To make it run for you, you have to observe the rules. The rules say that in conversation there is an *exchange*, part listening, part talking. To be a winner you have to be a good listener, not just a patient waiter enduring until it is your turn to perform again (or interrupting if your patience runs out).

To be a really top listener it's absolutely necessary that you be interested in other people. On the other hand, it will be very helpful to others if, when it is your turn to talk, you have something to say worth listening to.

Someone has said that the trouble with us young is that we have no conversation. That always reminds me of the story about the famous German author, Erich Maria Remarque, when he gave as a reason for not visiting the United States his lack of English. He knew only a few sentences which were: "How do you do? I love you. Forgive me. Forget me. Ham and eggs, please." And an American girl replied, "But with that vocabulary you could tour my country from Maine to California."

Maybe on tour, but no one, young or old, has any conversation who sticks to five sentences. It's a terrible teen-age temptation, though, because the truth is that while we really have plenty to say, we are too lazy to make the effort. We either rely on a few well-worn slang phrases, or we go to the other extreme and rely on telling the plot of a movie everyone has already seen, or jokes that are old, worn-out clinkers. Sometimes, too, we talk just to fill dead air. All this is fine up to a point. But look around you and notice that the really attractive personalities in your age group do have lively, new, interesting, conversation. Shirley always did and that was one reason things never bogged down where she was. I'll say this, too—she always had something good to say about somebody else. She has since told me she concentrated on it. She was a popular gal.

Here are a few do's and don'ts I'd advise if you really want to be fun to talk to.

Don't rely on five sentences.

Don't get completely carried away with "hep" talk (or any other speech novelty).

Do be brief, newsy, and pick a subject that might conceivably interest your partner in this game. This would mean that the hot-rod enthusiast would either pick a girl who's half grease-monkey or hold his talk of "milled head" to a minimum. A girl talking to a fellow wouldn't expect to interest him in how she makes "tailor's tacks."

Don't start a story or joke unless you can remember the end. (I've "bombed" quite a few times in that department.)

Don't be catty, or gossip, or talk entirely about yourself if you want to be well liked.

Above all, *don't* be afraid of silence if you have nothing to say. You can always whistle Dixie, or sing, or smile, or even listen. But the awful truth is that if we talk just to hear ourselves talking we usually wind up the only listener.

The single finest rule for conversation I know I saw on a sign in the office of a southern air base: "CAUTION—Be Sure Brain Is Engaged Before Putting Mouth Into Gear."

Daring to be yourself

One last word on friendship. It's normal for teen-agers to form social groups. This is fine and healthy if these are *circles of friendship*—based on the principles we have been discussing. It is quite another thing, to my mind, if they are mutual protective societies, cliques, crowds, threesomes or foursomes that use their united power to exclude or hurt others; or to give a group security to do things that not one of them would do as an individual; or to deprive members of individuality until they all follow leaders like sheep or insist on doing what "all the other girls do" simply because all the other girls do it.

I'm not talking about juvenile gangs either. I've actually seen a strong clique of supposedly nice girls pick the feathers from an outsider, or kick out some poor gal for failure to conform, or talk about an absent one in a way that made me wonder what little girls are made of.

I know this is all unusual but I think it's really important to guard against it happening at all. The basis of all happy social dealings is being kind to one another. I, for one, really admire the guys and gals who have the courage to insist on doing that. What I'm saying is, don't let any group become so important to you that you will betray your own standards to belong to it. Maybe that sounds like an odd way to tell you to make a hit, but believe me, you won't lose any friends. You may, however, find a few friends you didn't really know you had.

Look, I know this isn't easy. I have had my own problems along this line, like the question of joining a high school fraternity. To assume an air of exclusiveness, some frats discriminate against boys because of their poverty or belief or race. My parents disapproved of that, but when I pledged, intending to join a frat, they didn't forbid me. Something else did. It suddenly just seemed goofy, I guess, because it didn't stack up with the principles of friendship as I understood them. Now, it might coincide with your principles. Then it would be all right for you. But it wasn't for me. So I had to make a stand right there.

This doesn't mean defiance, or bitterness, or trying to tear others down. It just means the quiet courage to do what you think is right, and stand on the consequences, like the little boy whose Sunday school teacher asked: "If you are always kind and polite to all your playmates, what will they think of you?"

The boy said: "Some of them will think they can lick me."

And some of them will think they can lick you. But when they find that they can't, then the right ones will join you, and you will have taken the step that means leadership. You are bound to be attractive to worthwhile people because now you really have what it takes to be a friend.

7

"Someday You'll Understand"

Last summer, when we hiked out to Hollywood to make the motion picture *Mardi Gras*, we rented a great big house with a swimming pool and all the trimmings. Pretty terrific after the modest (and crowded) six room house we own in Leonia, New Jersey. It was to be a "work vacation." Of course the beautiful house was turned into a sick bay right off the bat when our four darling daughters promptly came down with measles. But when the last little spot disappeared we found that a pool can be a big social attraction.

One afternoon we had about fifty young people from church for a swimming party and barbecue before Wednesday night Prayer Meeting. Going to church meant taking along Lyn Carlton, our teen-age baby sitter from across the street in Leonia, who had come west with us for a short visit, and Judy Plumb, a seventeen-year-old member of the Church of Christ from Iowa, who was earning college tuition as Shirley's summer assistant. Of course, all supervising of our babies is "supervised" by Eva, who was nurse to Shirley and her three sisters. Still and all, having personally had the baby sitting detail for our four active young 'uns, I can tell you it isn't a one-man or one-woman job. If Shirley and I are ever to have a little time off together we need assistance from Lyn or Judy.

On the evening of our swimming party, after a noisy afternoon in the pool and a hilarious supper, we decided to take time off after church, just the two of us, to see a movie. (Married people *do* need time occasionally to do simple quiet things together like holding hands in the back row.)

The whole point is that, when church was over, we were in a hurry to get Lyn and Judy home and make the second show. The girls were talking to teen-age friends when we told them we were ready to leave. They nodded agreeably. They are nice, polite, well-behaved girls. But when we looked back from the door they were still talking—and when we got to the car, guess what? They hadn't moved an inch.

"What can they possibly have left to say when they've been together since three this afternoon?" Shirley demanded.

I was wondering the same thing and feeling a little annoyed when suddenly I heard a voice from the past, Shirley's dad, asking the same thing about us. I mentioned this to Shirley and added, "Mama used to say that, too."

"Well," said my wife, looking at her watch, "this is different."

Then I had to laugh. "Sure it's different. Now we're the grown-ups!"

We both grinned and Shirley chuckled, "Well, I understand now *why* they said it," and walked off to physically collar the girls.

It was sort of a stunning moment for me, though, because I remember another conversation with my mother. It was when my rosiest dream was to possess a Whizzer motor bike and my parents said "no." I thought they were pretty mean and they thought they were kind since it was a matter of my safety. We had a little pow-wow, not much though, because when my family said "no" they meant N-O. Afterward Mama said, "Someday you'll understand . . ."

And now, in just a few short years, that "someday" had arrived, and in a few more I'd be saying to Cherry, and Lindy, and Debby, and Laury, "some day you'll understand" (because if Cherry was that same age right today I wouldn't let *her* have a Whizzer!). You see, it's a cycle. Round and round, generation to generation, parent-to-teen-agers-to-parent-to-teen-agers.

I know we say, when we're on the receiving end, "I'll let *my* children have Whizzers, and horses, and cars, and paint their fingernails red, and stay out 'til two," but when the time comes and we understand, we change our minds. Believe me!

Mark Twain, the great American writer, summed this idea up pretty neatly. "When I was a boy of fourteen," he said, "my father was so ignorant I could hardly stand to have the old man around. But when I got to be twenty-one, I was astonished at how much the old man had learned in seven years."

It is astonishing, I can tell you, to begin to understand your parents. It is also a little sad. For you realize that most of the trouble, the friction and heartache, comes because we don't try to understand each other at the time.

Me, I've got one foot on each side of the dividing line and I get a first class view of both sides. I think that the largest percentage of teen-agers have intelligent, sensible relations with intelligent, sensible parents. This is a great blessing. On the other hand, when there is friction at home, I think this can be one of the single most difficult parts of the teen age for all parties concerned. Some parent says to me, "I'm going to lose my mind if Junior (or Nancy) doesn't stop. . . ." And then letters come in from the offspring saying: "My parents simply won't understand me. I'm about to lose my mind. . . ."

To tell the truth neither of them ever does, quite. But I've seen everybody get pretty shook up, and a lot of suffering both ways, everything from tears, tantrums, sarcasm, nagging, silent sulks, to real nasty fights and kids leaving home. It ain't civilized! Just between you and me, it isn't any fun and it doesn't get anybody anywhere.

Where does the fault lie? Usually a little on both sides, but you can waste a lot of time trying to decide who's to blame when what really matters is deciding how to lessen the friction and made life as pleasant as possible.

Now what is the best way to get along with parents, since they can be useful around the house? Granted, it can take a little doing sometimes. But let's see if we can figure it out together.

How to get along with normal parents

The trouble with even the most normal parents from the average teen-age point of view is that they worry too much. They have various ways of showing it, but by and large they worry because we aren't popular; about our homework; over whether or not we'll ever learn to be neat, or prompt, or dependable; over whether we'll "get into trouble" somehow. They worry if we do the same things they did, or they worry if we don't do them. They are afraid we won't take advantage of all the opportunities they missed. Most of all they seem constantly worried about our safety. All this makes them say "no" to a lot of things.

From our viewpoint as teen-agers we figure if we're old enough to be given the responsibility for baby sitting, cleaning house, doing the family shopping, driving cars, solving complicated problems in physics or algebra (and getting an A sometimes) why aren't we old enough to decide for ourselves things like what hour we will come home? If we're late it throws them into a tizzy of concern which we can't understand. We know where we were and that we were all

right. We can take care of ourselves. Nothing is going to
happen to us. Why all the worry? Even with kind, sensible,
normal parents, and this is the kind I had, we sense some
kind of injustice here.

In our house it was Mama who sat up in her rocking chair
waiting 'til I came in. My mother, as I've already said, has a
low boiling point sometimes, a temper that flares quickly,
and if I was a little late, and worried her only a little, it
sputtered up like a match and went out. But if I was a lot
late, as has been known to happen, and she worried a lot,
her relief at seeing me all in one piece didn't put out the
three-alarm fire that flared when she thought of the needless anxiety I'd put her through. Talk about "Yakkety-
Yak!"

I muttered to myself about "mothers" and "women" and
I admit that I often resented this concern until one night
when Mama was in Jacksonville visiting her folks and
Daddy was left in charge. Well, I didn't give myself any
trouble about getting in on time that night. I figured Daddy
was a sensible man and would go peacefully to bed because
he always got up at five-thirty or six every A.M. to spend an
hour preparing for his very popular Sunday school class.
Anyway, it was one-thirty when Don Henley and I drove
up to my house and saw a light still burning downstairs.
This wasn't in the script so Don parked on down a way, and
I sneaked back to look around.

Just as I pushed my face against the window to see what
was doing inside, my dad pushed his face against it to look
outside for signs of his wandering boy—and there we were,
nose to nose. I tell you that sudden intimate view of Daddy's
worried face startled me so that I yelped and ran halfway
back to Don's car. But of course I just had to turn around
and go inside and face what was coming.

It wasn't much. Daddy wasn't a great one for fireworks.
He explained that with Mama away the responsibility for

Homework.

GARY WAGNER

On time for class.

GARY WAGNER

Art for Art's sake.

AT COLUMBIA

GARY WAGNER

Concentration.

GARY WAGNER

School's Out!

The great day (*left to right:* Marge Jenks Boone, Shirley,
Pat, Mama, Dad, Sister Judy).

THE PAT BOONES
ABROAD
London and Paris

Rehearsing with Tab Hunter.

Serenade.

Love Letters in the Sand.

So long for now.

seeing that I was safely in fell on him. That Mama usually did it, not because women worry more, but because she felt it was part of her job and he needed sleep. He then said there would always be one of them waiting up for me.

It was just as he started off to bed that he turned and said the few words that suddenly threw light for me on the whole situation. "You see, Pat," he said simply, "we care."

There was the answer to that question, "Why all the worrying?" It was *"We care!"* I know you've heard this same thing over and over, just like I had, but it takes hearing a thing lots of times for it, all of a sudden, to soak in!

Most of the rules parents make, whether we think them right or wrong, don't stem from meanness, or narrow-mindedness, or wanting to spoil our fun. They are made because our parents care what happens to us. Once I understood that, I hated to see teen-agers hold it against Mom and Dad for worrying about them doing something dangerous or something they think unwise.

Maybe you've already thought "if they really loved me, they'd want me to have what makes me happy (like a Whizzer or a horse or a car) and let me do as I please as long as I'm not doing anything wrong (like staying at a party until one-thirty if we're having a good time)." I'd thought that way myself.

But it just isn't so. Believe me, it would be a lot easier to let us have our own way—and win nothing but smiles from us. I know this already from that one foot I've got over in parenthood.

It costs parents something to stick by their guns for your welfare!

Before Cherry was a year old we found out that even small children can want things that look harmless but aren't good for them. Shirley and I made a pretty good start at spoiling this little jewel before she could walk. Because of us, she grew to want and expect attention all the time. The doctor said that wasn't good for her physically and would ruin her disposition, besides. His exact words were, "They need love but not coddling" and we were instructed to undo what we had begun and "let her cry it out."

Well, you should have seen us sitting in our tiny living room in Denton holding a debate while our first-born howled her head off in the next room. We had put her down with a full stomach, checked for pins and excess moisture, but still every few minutes one or the other of us would bust through that door to "take a look." A couple of times Shirley gave in and picked her up—being rewarded with an instantaneous rainbow smile.

"I must love her more than you do," Cherry's mother would say. "I just can't stand to let her cry."

"And I love her more than you do," I'd argue, "because I can let her cry even when it hurts me, if it's for her own good." But the funny part is, when Shirley wasn't looking, I sneaked in and picked up the little squealer, too.

I still hold to that view, though. I have some proof, too. Cherry got over howling for attention.

And here's a teen-age case. A mother I know in California was having a good deal of a hassle with her rugged thirteen-year-old son about homework. Finally she decreed that he had to come straight home after school and could not go out and play ball until the homework was finished. One afternoon her son came in and announced with a triumphant grin, "Well, you won't be able to make me do my homework today. We're supposed to write a tribute to Mother for Mother's Day and even you won't force me to pay you one."

"You're only half right," said his mother. "You can write anything about me you like, but you're going to do your homework. I happen to like you well enough to see that you do what's right even if it hurts me."

Well, there was a lot of dark muttering, but "A Tribute to Mother," by George Kennahan, got him an "A" in school and was purchased and published by Guideposts Magazine where I first saw it. George is in the Army now, in Germany, and Army discipline wasn't the shock to him that it is to some guys because his mother stuck by her guns. This homework essay shows how much we can understand about our parents if we really try, even at thirteen. Here's what George wrote:

PERSONALLY I'M GLAD I'LL NEVER BE A MOTHER *

If a boy turns out a bad citizen it reflects on his mother.

There is a time in every boy's life when you think your mother is nothing but a traffic cop because she will not let you have all the freedom you want.

My mother always says, "You are lucky I was a child before I was a mother." By this I think she means she knows what we are going through and wants to set us straight before someone else does, someone who might not be so sympathetic.

If your mother is a praying woman, that's good. Because then you learn to pray too, and there are times when you sure need to know how. If she is a real Christian you are lucky. Then she will probably practice what she preaches which seems very hard for most people. My mother is both a praying woman and a Christian.

This has some difficulties too. She is dynamite on the Ten Commandments . . . but she says if we practice those long enough we can drop them and only use the two Jesus gave, "Love the Lord thy God" . . . and "love thy neighbor." If you really use those you couldn't break the others. At the moment I am still stuck with the Ten Commandments.

Mothers never even get a day off and don't even have a minimum wage. There is no Mother's Union to protect her from long hours, hard work, and order a vacation with pay. Therefore I think we should give our mothers all the respect we can and not only on Mother's Day.

Personally I am very glad I will never be a mother.

Here are a few concrete suggestions I'd offer for getting along with normal parents.

* Copyright 1954 by Guideposts Associates, Inc. Published at Carmel, N.Y.

ONE: *Try a little empathy:* Now there's a great word. It isn't sympathy misspelled. Empathy means doing what young Kennahan did . . . imaginative projection of one's own consciousness into another's. Simplified, it means putting yourself in the other guy's shoes and trying to see and feel as he does in order to understand him better. It can be done, although 'tain't easy! That night when my daddy said "We care!" I had a moment of complete empathy. I could feel what they felt sitting up there patiently waiting either for me to come home or for the phone to ring. It doesn't mean I agreed necessarily (any more than Kennahan decided he'd like to be a mother, which was fortunate for him under the circumstances), but it did mean a lot less resentment and a lot more understanding.

It's been my experience that you never can handle any situation that involves other people if you react strictly from your own limited viewpoint. To reach a harmonious solution always requires trying to see the other guy's side. With parents this means trying to talk things over with them a little more reasonably. Sometimes we clam up, and the minute communication ceases between us, neither side can be expected to understand. Empathy is easier than mind reading. So give it a try!

TWO; *Give your parents credit for having once been young:* For the record, they had to be teen-agers at some time. If you think they've forgotten it, try to recall it by asking questions about their youth (not sarcastic questions, but honest, interested ones!). Discuss what they thought, did, what problems they faced, how their parents handled them. You'd be surprised at how few teen-agers do that. It may give you a clue on why you are being handled as you are, and to what they are thinking and feeling regarding your teen age. So listen to what they say.

Usually some place in this region of the past is the explanation as to why they want you to be "popular," or play the piano, or football, or learn fancy embroidery. Sometimes prohibitions are based on mistakes they made, and being pushed is based on things they wanted to do but never got a chance—or even on the fact that they want you to be a replica of themselves so they can live these years all over again.

Once you have got your clue, you can then explain that you are a different teen-ager, differently equipped, and with different aims; that no two people were ever created alike and that these are the things that interest you. If you can touch a memory chord while you are both thinking in these teen-age terms there will be a closeness and understanding that cannot happen any other way.

THREE: *Dime Insurance:* This is a simple, practical step that works wonders with worried parents (Of course it can be overworked but you know that). In our circle it started with a mother who had once worked on a newspaper. A newspaper "must" is to call the city desk after every assignment. She said one of the most interesting things she learned was that there were telephones all over town—in movie houses, gas stations, drive-ins, private homes, schools—that any child of ten could learn to use.

When her son went out she handed him a dime to put in his shoe. "Now that is *my* dime," she'd say. "It is to be used only to call me. You get impatient with me because I worry when you say you are perfectly all right. Well, then let me in on the secret. If you call me on the dot, or a few minutes before you are due home, tell me where you are, how much longer within reason you expect to be, I'll give you that much grace because I won't worry." It worked so well a lot of guys and gals adopted this method. It's another case of courtesy or consideration for others oiling the machinery of good human relations.

FOUR: *Try to imagine life with a different set of parents:* I actually knew a pair of girls once who exchanged parents for a brief period. Each had been singing the virtues of the other's parents at home—"Ronnie's mother lets *her* . . ." and "Sarah's mother *never* . . ."—until the mothers met and compared notes at a PTA meeting. These very intelligent women decided to let the girls have a taste of what the other's home life was like. You can imagine what happened. Two disillusioned girls came home dragging their tails behind them after finding out that every home has restrictions and no parents are perfect by any teen-age yardstick.

After I heard about this, I tried in my imagination moving in with the various parents of my friends, and . . . well, I decided I'd stick to the ones I had. I was used to 'em. Besides . . . they *cared,* and this simple experiment showed me that *so did I.*

How to get along with extreme parents

We've been talking about average, normal, parents, and average, normal, teen-agers. Now let's admit that, just as teen-agers can go to extremes, so can parents. The most common extremes are: Too Strict, and Too Lenient.

Granted we rarely hear complaints about the Too Lenient parents until their children have grown up and are muddled and confused by a big, big, world in which they do not seem to know the rules for happy living.

The Too Lenient parents can be recognized pretty early. They don't want any trouble, or anything but "love" and "harmony" in their home—like the nervous papa who said to his very active, noisy, son, "Sit down!"

And the young man replied, "I won't!"

So his father said, "Very well, then stand up. I *will* be obeyed!"

This type of parent does not find the arrival of the teens hard on them at all. I've known some of their offspring, and when they hit thirteen or fourteen their parents are delighted to believe that now their children can really look after themselves. If you drew these happy-go-lucky parents, don't pat yourself on the back too fast. It simply means you'll probably have to work double time. I've watched these kids without rules, guidance, anchors, or for that matter, anyone cheering in their corner either. They've had to take full responsibility for *self* discipline at a very early age. It's rough. But it has to be done or they'll be losers from now on.

The best suggestion I can offer if you find that you are being left on your own without too much guidance from home is to pick the girls or boys you most admire and try to find the rules they live by. Keep your family loyalty even if sometimes you don't think it's deserved, and work double time on your maturity chart. You really have to do-it-yourself.

Too Strict parents either literally don't remember their own youth at all, or seem to remember it too well with distaste and fear. If your parents are genuinely too strict (and in your heart of hearts you will probably know the truth about this) you'll have to redouble your efforts at empathy to try to understand why. Meanwhile, no strict parent was ever won over to seeing your side of things by defiance, disobedience, or a comparative description of what "all the other parents" do.

You will have to work double time to convince them of your trustworthiness and common sense. Do what you can to show by your actions and the reasonableness of your desires, plus the way you execute their present orders, that you are the kind of young person who can be trusted. When you are tempted to resist violently, remember what happens to a large dog wearing one of those choke collars. The harder the dog struggles and pulls, the tighter the collar gets. It's no joke. The neck you save may be your own!

Try to relax and go along with the situation for now,

knowing that unlike your opposite number with the easy-going parents, the only way you can get really off the beam is by letting resentment fester in you, or by straining at the leash until you strangle. Oh, sure, you may lose out on some fun, but you'll gain in the long run. Parents can learn, too!

Problem parents and problem children

One of the boys who came to our swimming party had a tragic history. At Christmas time the year before, his father was killed in a drunken barroom brawl. His mother was in jail, and he and his younger brother and sister were living in foster homes.

We'll call him Tom, but that is not his name. Tom is fourteen and looks sixteen or seventeen. With his background, if he had wound up in juvenile court it would not have surprised anyone. But he didn't. Tom is a wonderful guy, quiet, dependable, well liked, a pretty good student.

Now, he didn't get his rules of living from his parents. Even if they had offered good ones Tom would have been suspicious. "Do-as-I-say-and-not-as-I-do" is poor bait for landing teen-agers. Yet Tom has literally taken himself in hand and "brought himself up." He is a fine young guy and will be a fine man. We talked a little about how he had done it, alone, and with every human excuse for lapsing into the pattern called "juvenile delinquency."

"Well," Tom said, "I took a good look at the people around me, and it wasn't too hard to decide which were the happy ones. I'd seen how my folks wound up and it didn't look good to me. I noticed that a lot of the excitement the guys were getting into wound up about the same way. The happiest people I found were these Church of Christ people, so I stayed close to them. I've tried to do what they do, and what they told me to do. When things went real wrong . . ." He chokes up when he tries to talk about what happened to his parents. "I was ashamed to face anybody. I, well, I kinda hurt inside. But they came and, gee, they were real great!"

You see, even when things are real wrong at home, even when you hurt inside, you still don't have to become a problem child. You *can* find happiness for yourself.

Broken homes, drunkenness, fights, delinquent parents can be made excuses for becoming a problem child if you want to use them. But the choice is yours. Always! Teen-agers from such backgrounds have turned out to be fine, gifted people when they made the right choice. There are a lot of Toms in this world right now. And teen-agers from good, normal, homes have wound up in police court while some over-privileged homes can be the worst of all. I've seen them!

If you have not always had advantages, a sound example, the feeling of being cared for and about, don't give up! I understand your temptation to bitterness, to shame, the loneliness, the what's-the-use attitude. I know it's asking a lot of you to overcome them, but, hang it all, I know that if you yield you will have an unhappy life! The first thing to remember is that you are not alone. There are a lot of people who care. I know. I'm one of them!

A physician in Atlanta, Georgia, once made a statement I thought terrific. "An adolescent," said Dr. William H. Kiser, Jr., "often is a segregated individual (lonely, apart). He needs a bridge to the adult world. The very best way to provide that bridge is through the mother and father. I like to explain it as if these kids are like moths attracted to something that glows. If the father doesn't 'glow,' the youngster will attach himself to someone else—sometimes to a psychopathic teen-ager who 'glows' in an evil way. That's how teen-age gangs are formed."

It's well worth while for every teen-ager to think about this "glowing." We are the lucky ones if our parents "glow" for us. We have some responsibility, too, when we realize that we might glow for someone else. But if that glow is not present in your home, you aren't beaten!

Not unless you let yourself be attracted to the wrong flame. Tom has found his "glow" in the church, in the good people who've taken an interest in him, in a happy way of life, and he has stuck close to that warmth.

If you are one of the unhappy ones with a real problem at home, there is still no reason why you can't become a sound person, even a better person than the rest of us, because I have seen tremendous mental and spiritual muscles develop very young where the teen-ager has had to make this greater effort. Certainly you are the one who has to make the effort, but there are ministers, teachers, youth leaders, young people in church, and youth groups who would consider it a privilege to help you.

Let them! And God bless you.

8

Your Personal Gold Mine

My first business venture was at the age of nine, selling buttercups on Granny White Pike near our house. I got the buttercups for nothing because they grew in our own front yard. Mama let me gather them and tie them in big bunches and then I'd stand on the corner and look hopeful, but when people stopped I never could bring myself to name a price. I'd say, "Whatever you want to pay." . . . I suspect now that I made more this way, as much some afternoons as a dollar.

My second effort was singing at the Belle Meade Theater "Happiness Club" and it was worth one banana split per appearance. Ed Jordan, an ex-vaudevillian, manages this theater in Nashville and every Saturday he holds a talent contest. I don't know how it works now, but it used to be that you auditioned up town at the Elizabeth Bryant Combs Dance Studio and seven or eight kids were picked to come and perform at the Saturday matinees.

From the time I first won when I was ten, until I was thirteen, I sang at those matinees pretty regularly. Every other

Saturday, to be exact. Looking back, I believe it was the toughest assignment I ever had. The audience yelled and threw
popcorn and spit wads at each other until Mr. Jordan came
out and threatened to eject them . . . and all the time I
was singing away, entertaining nobody but myself, and all
for banana splits. I will say this, though, that no young Bing
Crosby or Ann Miller ever had a better friend than Ed Jordan.

I couldn't bear to charge for my flowers, and musically,
until I was fourteen years old, I never lost my amateur standing.

Then why was I singing and selling buttercups?

If you asked the first ten grown-ups you meet why they
work, eight out of ten would probably look at you as if
you'd flipped and say, "Why, for money," or "Because I
have to, junior!"

Maybe they think that's true. And if it is, it's too bad.
Don't get me wrong. I'm very thankful for every penny I'm
paid. (I'd say an extra "Thanks" if I could *keep* a few of
them!) And certainly the workman is worthy of his hire.
We'll go into that later. But the point I am making here is
that these weren't the real *reasons* I started to work. And it
probably isn't the reason you did your first jobs.

Do you remember when you were so young that it was a
big treat if your mom let you help with the dishes or cook or
push the vacuum? Or your dad let you have a hand in wash-
ing his car? I do. Certainly we didn't *have* to do it (I suspect
now our parents were being patient when they let us get
our sticky fingers in the pie) and we certainly didn't get
paid. Then why were we such eager beavers?

Wasn't it because we wanted to be a part of the life going
on around us, a necessary, active part? I think we all have
the instinct to work, and at that point we didn't fight it.
Admit it now . . . we thought it was fun!

Admit, too, that we'd all be a lot happier if we didn't become the type of grown-up who complains, and protests his work as something he does because he *has to* in order to earn money. Where and when do we lose that youthful joyous instinct? That wanting to work for the fun of it? Because somewhere along the line an awful lot of young people do lose it.

This was noticed by no less an authority than a famous president of the United States. Here's a letter written by a great man who knew a good bit about hard manual labor, to a Major Ramsey:

> Executive Mansion,
> Oct. 17, 1861.

My Dear Sir:

The lady bearer of this says she has two sons who want to work. Set them at it if possible. Wanting to work is so rare a want that it should be encouraged.

> Yours truly,
>
> A. Lincoln

All right then, what *does* change our early enthusiasm into the Big Groan (or a little shriveled-up groan depending on our personality type)?

We suddenly, as teen-agers, begin to have responsibilities—work we have to do which we haven't chosen.

Let's be honest. I chose to sell buttercups and to sing. You probably chose to play in the hose helping dad wash his car on a hot day or to try to make cup cakes. Then comes the time when we simply help with the dishes, clean house, pull weeds, milk cows, because it's there to be done *right now* and we're elected, unanimously. So we rebel. We don't wanna.

And right at this point we can lose our taste for work forever if we aren't careful. But at this same point we *may* take our first steps toward ultimate success in life. Because, you remember, we'll always be idle dreamers if we don't know how to back our dreams with effort.

No matter what you pick to do in later life, even if it's the thing you love best, you'll find it entails some distasteful but essential work.

I love making movies, for instance. But I don't love long hours on a hot set rehearsing the same scene over and over and over, or having my face made up over a sunburn or taking the dad-burned stuff off any time! I won't even mention the work that goes into TV—I get backaches just thinking about it. Eddie Le Baron likes to play pro football, but during the season this means about an eighty hour week, calisthenics twice a day, hours of chalk talk, heavy drill, scrimmage, tackling dummies . . . and all for sixty minutes or less of actual play. That's work, man!

Our own success in life will depend upon learning the discipline of doing the work at hand (chores, homework, housework, whatever, and however distasteful) during the teen age. Honest! Boy. I'm surprised at how easy it is for me to tell you all this, considering how tough it was for me to do it myself!

But if we don't learn to apply ourselves to distasteful as well as pleasant jobs we'll probably turn out to be just sort of idle dreamers—like the Maine farmer who had been telling a summer visitor that for ten years he had dreamed of turning his land into a model farm. When the visitor looked out all he saw were rocks. "How do they happen to be here?" the visitor asked. "Glacier brought 'em," said the farmer. What was he going to do about it? asked the visitor. "Wait for another glacier to take 'em away," was the answer.

My friend, I hope your attitude toward work is different from his. Glaciers are few and far between.

We learn to work by working. Can you think of another way? If so, please write me care of this station!

We have to consider learning to work *today* as training

for *the* job we will want to do someday. It has helped me, for instance, to imagine that mowing the yard was a scene in a movie or that milking the cow was shaking hands with a famous celebrity—good imagination, huh?

We talk ourselves out of our enjoyment of work because of popular opinion. Griping is supposedly the thing to do! But is it right if we sell ourselves the idea that work is a burden? I've heard girls who actually love to cook and were terrific cooks, too, complaining that they *had* to get dinner on a certain night, in order to get sympathy from their girl friends. Or a fellow who actually loved gardening beefing to the guys that he had to go prune his mom's roses because he didn't want them to think he enjoyed it. Maybe you *like* algebra homework. Don't talk yourself out of it. You may be a potentially great teacher! Or even a TV quiz winner!

We do not make the important connection between our presence here on earth and the things we were put here to do.

This, to me, is absolutely top priority if we're to live happy, successful lives—if we are to reach maturity, that full development of our all round potential.

Here is a thought I'd like to offer you. You might even read it over twice to get the full gist—it's worth it! It was written by Kahlil Gibran in a small book called *The Prophet*:

"*Always you have been told that work is a curse and labour a misfortune.*

"*But I say to you that when you work you fulfill a part of earth's furthest dream, assigned to you when that dream was born. . . .*" *

* Reprinted from *The Prophet*, by Kahlil Gibran, with permission of the publisher, Alfred A. Knopf, Inc. Copyright 1923 by Kahlil Gibran; renewal copyright 1951 by Administrators C.T.A. of Kahlil Gibran Estate and Mary G. Gibran.

Isn't that a great idea? Doesn't that show that our instinct as kids toward work was right? But it also makes finding our *right work,* finding what we as individuals are best fitted to do, a sacred thing.

How to find your talent

When you find the right work for you, you've found your gold mine in the sky. One of the most exciting and challenging things about the teen age is that this is where the search usually begins.

How do we go about finding it?

I've known a lucky few who just knew straight off. So have you. One of my buddies decided when he was eight that he was going to be a doctor. He went toward his goal straight as an arrow and today he is interning in a big hospital. A girl in our town knew at the age of ten that she wanted to be a writer. She wrote all the time, everything from horrible novels to a penny newspaper of neighborhood happenings. Later she was on the high school paper and began doing a teen-age column for the local sheet. Today she combines newspaper work and homemaking with good success, although she has to work hard to keep up with both jobs.

For most of us, though (including me), it doesn't come like a bolt from the blue. We go hustling from one interest to another like nervous bees. We have hobbies that may turn into a lifetime profession or, as was mostly my case, fizzle out just about when we get all the equipment paid for. Our parents shake their heads at a microscope or butterfly net or a five pound lump of professional modeling clay lying abandoned in our room. However, this is *part* of how we find our true talent. We follow our interests and instincts until we know what we do well, and what we don't do well, what we like and what we don't like.

Another thing, we usually identify ourselves with every profession that is presented to us even in movies and television. At least I did. If I spent time with the friend who was going to be a doctor, I went home and dreamed of myself in surgery. Like "Medic," you know. If our physics teacher got lost in descriptions of how to build a bridge, or I saw a movie about an explorer, I alternated in my daydreams between being a great engineer and climbing Mt. Everest. We teen-agers try everything on for size in our imagination. And this is good, except during class.

Then usually we do some actual apprentice work. Girls who are active on the social side of their charts serve the community as nurses' aides, or junior camp counselors, or take care of children, or like me, they serve an apprenticeship in school politics.

My own experience was a mixture of all these things and more. I loved comic books and had huge stacks of them carefully preserved because I figured that in fifty or sixty years they'd be collectors' items and make me rich. By the time I was twelve I was drawing my own comic strips, and in high school I was both a reporter and cartoonist on the paper. I dallied with the idea of making one of these hobbies my life's work.

Meanwhile, from my fourteenth to my nineteenth summer I was an actual apprentice learning a trade in the Boone Construction Company. Daddy started both Nick and me as carpenter's helpers at seventy-five cents an hour. His orders were that we were to learn to work, and learn to take orders. By the second summer we were laborers at eighty cents an hour, then ninety-five and eventually we worked up to one dollar. And I do mean *worked* up. It didn't take me long to decide against construction work as my career— but many guys enjoy it, and many like my Dad have had happy and successful lives in this business.

Singing was another of my hobbies. Sure, I had dreams about it. But I was full of dreams. However I was also actively experimenting. When I was about fourteen I lost my amateur standing when a man gave me $5.00 to sing some western and pop numbers at a Kiwanis Club dinner. From then on I alternated between singing for free meals and singing for a few dollars at Kiwanis or Lions or Shakespeare clubs and it didn't matter to me which I got.

I also entered every contest that came to town. Mama began to think that perhaps this was getting more time than a hobby should. When Horace Heidt and his band arrived in Nashville offering a contest in which the winner would go on the road with them, we had a serious discussion. Mama was worried. She thought I might want to go but since I lost twice, it was no problem.

In fact, I lost and lost. After the first couple of contests I honestly didn't expect to win. I kept on because it was fun. Then I was offered a real job with a good local band. I talked that one over with my friend Mack Craig. It meant late hours, a chance of goofing at school, and singing for dances. I wasn't happy about any of these things.

So Mack went out and helped me get my first radio show going instead. It was "Youth on Parade" on station WSIX. The owner of the station was Louis Draughon, the man who gave me that first paying job after Shirley and I were married. The program director and my first guide on radio was Jim McKinney. But "Youth on Parade" didn't pay at all. Not even banana splits. I was the emcee, host, and occasional singer on this for two years, my senior year in high and my freshman year in college. Why? Because it was fun! I enjoyed the work. I was also learning more about a possible profession.

But by this time the possibilities were narrowing down. I had abandoned medicine, engineering, exploring, cartooning (at least temporarily), reporting, and sundry other things. I felt personally drawn to only three: teaching (English or Speech preferred), educational TV, and singing.

(The order is based on likelihood of occurrence, not preference.)

I think that's about par for the average teen-ager. When we hit college we've narrowed down—some more, some less. Perhaps you're still not entirely sure, but at least the indications are strong enough so that you can concentrate on the few that have stood the withering test of teen-age investigation. There'll be lots of trained people to help you proceed. There are even tests given in high school for your vocational aptitude.

But may I give you a few mild words of warning?

In this matter, your own heart and head must decide. *This is a choice that has to come from within.* You shouldn't pick your life's work for some outside reason, such as qualifying in a test or doing what your Dad and Mom have always wanted you to be, or becoming a banker because all bankers have wall-to-wall carpets. If you *do* choose for outside reasons, there's no guarantee you'll be happy in your work. Successful, perhaps, in a business way. But with ulcers yet, maybe. Because many financially successful people are the very ones who say crossly that the only reason they work is to earn money. And that's not successful living.

Another warning. If you are not beginning to zero in on a career by your senior year in high school, do some honest checking. There is danger of your becoming a permanently nervous bee, liking things only when they are new and fresh, and not liking them when it comes time to buckle down and get on with it. You don't want to wind up in a quandary like this many-legged friend:

A centipede was happy quite,
Until a frog, in fun,
Said "Pray which leg comes after which?"
This raised her mind to such a pitch
She lay distracted in the ditch,
Considering how to run.

But if you do find yourself, as I did, with several equally appealing prospects, go ahead with them all until you are sure. You won't lose anything. Girls who have lovely voices and choose motherhood can still sing. They add to any church group, amateur theatricals, clubs and youth activities. If you can't have a ceramics studio because you have a big family, you'll shine helping youngsters earn scout badges. Typing can be an asset in a wife for any husband. My mother's nurses' training certainly came in handy around our household. She saved my life more than once.

Don't neglect any talent. It's a Divine gift. Our part is to develop it!

To sum up: The three chief ways to find your talent are first, to pursue your hobbies actively (sports included); second, use your imagination to try on various professions that appeal to you—back this up with reading, study, and talking to people already engaged in them; third, do some actual apprentice work where you can (even if it's only sweeping out floors) in fields that look attractive to you.

These items, plus a vow to *do the things at hand and learn to work,* should go on your maturity chart. Remember what another young writer named Solomon wrote: "Whatsoever thy hands find to do, do it with thy might." Finding your talent is opening the door to creativity, but *work* is what turns creativity into accomplishment.

How to follow your talent

The surest way I know to follow your talent is to have enthusiasm. Now most of us start off with a great blaze of this priceless stuff—and then it burns down to embers and finally ashes. How can we protect the flame?

We can recognize the truth that no talent is small. A girl with a talent for typing or homemaking belittles what she can do and thinks that it would be greater in the sight of God and her friends if she had the talent of Lily Pons or Helen

Hayes. But this isn't true. On what basis do we make such a comparison?

Believe me, your own talent, well-used and perfected, is equally great. A perfect orchid, a perfect rose, or a perfect daisy has each reached the real beauty of full development. Our ability to see this has to do with our attitude toward the whole pattern of living. Lily Pons' accompanist, each man in the orchestra behind her, each electrician and technician working backstage, is necessary and important to her performance.

There is a wonderful story told about Sir Christopher Wren, one of England's greatest architects, walking one day unrecognized among the men who were building St. Paul's cathedral in London which he had designed. He stopped and asked one of the workmen: "What are you doing?" "Anyone can see I'm cutting stone," the man said, grumpily. He asked another and was told, "I am earning five shilling twopence a day." But the third man he asked said: "I am helping Sir Christopher Wren build a great cathedral."

This man could see beyond cutting stone, beyond earning his daily living, to his actual talent, which was to assist in the creation of a work of art. This, to me, is the secret of happy living!

Does someone think that a talent for typing is a lowly one compared to the talent of the boss? Here's what one boss, Paul Dehn, thought about that:

```
My typist has gone on hir holiday
    My tipyst has gohn on a spree.
Mx typish hap gone oh hyr haliduy,
    O gring bacq m! hypist to me.
        Bling bac? oK §ring back
Oh bynK b4cK my tipisth to mi tu mo.
        Brung bicq ocsling 8acK
Oh blynK ba"K mg t#pys? tp m/
```

Or you think "Occupation: Housewife" requires *less* talent than going out to make a living? Here's what a breadwinner had to say after exchanging places with a homemaker:

> Mother wanted to shop; and father, a statistician, agreed to spend the afternoon with their three small children. On the return of mother, father handed her the following statement:
>
> "Dried tears—9 times; tied shoes—10 times; toy balloons purchased—3 per child; average life of balloon—12 seconds; cautioned children not to cross street—20 times; children insisted on crossing street—30 times; number of Saturdays father will do this again—0 times."

Whatever your talent is, regard it as something special and necessary, and you'll add fuel to the fire of enthusiasm.

Don't be afraid to fail: If you are, you'll never try anything new, or anything challenging, and you'll be stuck in the same old rut. Charles Kettering, for many years president of the General Motors Research Corporation, once said: "I can take any group of young people any place, and teach them to be inventors, if I can get them to throw off the hazards of being afraid to fail. You fail because your ideas aren't right. You shouldn't be afraid to fail, but you should learn to fail intelligently. By that I mean, when you fail, find out why you failed, and each time you fail it will bring you up nearer to your goal."

This is to fail successfully! This will spike discouragement! Look, I know how embarrassing it is to goof or flop—I've done it plenty of times. But when that happens, I try again, a little smarter. I recommend this to you.

Have Confidence in Yourself: This doesn't mean to develop a giant ego and go wild. It means not being afraid to take a chance—not being afraid of change. It means following your own honest dreams instead of settling for some second-hand ones others may have for you. It means living enthusiastically instead of settling for a pattern of mediocre material security.

Let me show you how necessary this was in my case. If I'd been afraid to take a chance I'd probably be sitting in Denton, Texas, today doing odd jobs, still wondering what to do with my life. In fact, I wouldn't even have made it to Denton in the first place.

You see I finally *did* win a contest—my first—in the spring of my freshman year at David Lipscomb college. It was the East Nashville Hi Talent Contest. The prize was a trip to New York, all expenses paid, and an audition for Ted Mack's Amateur Hour on TV. Never was a winner more surprised than I, and even though I went on to New York that summer and was on the show three times, qualifying for the finals the next summer, this really didn't seem encouragement enough to believe that singing was my life's work. I dreamed —but I went on with the studies that would qualify me some-day for teaching. That next summer, when I went back for the Ted Mack finals, I was a married man with a baby on the way, and while I not only appeared on the Amateur Hour but also auditioned for the Arthur Godfrey show, and ap-peared on that, right there my singing career seemed to come to a dead end. I had a couple of night club offers, but nothing that would do for a young family man named Boone.

On my way back to Denton I stopped in Nashville to see the folks. A disc jockey pal, Hugh Cherry, thought that, maybe now, Randy Wood, of Dot records, who lived in nearby Gallatin, might be interested in me. Well, you can't say my enthusiasm was dampened by failure. I had made some records once for a little label called Republic and we sold exactly eighty-five copies to all my relatives. I never got a cent because we didn't make enough to pay for the session.

Undaunted I went over to see Randy and we made a verbal contract for one year. As soon as he got a song he'd send for me. But he warned me it might take four to six weeks. That sounded like eternity! And when it turned out to be eight months I'd about given up.

When Randy's call finally came I was making a nifty $44.50 a week with WPAB-TV in Ft. Worth; I was doing fine in school; I was the proud papa of one small girl, another baby was on the way, and we had the beginning of a secure life. I might add, though, that a sizable investment in a pair of chinchillas which were to make our fortune had cleaned out our savings, and if I went to Chicago for that recording session I'd have to borrow bus fare. Either that, or limber up my thumb.

Well, there it was. Should I take the chance? Or should I settle for the security of the moment? Shirley, my parents, Mack Craig, all believed in me. But did I believe in myself? If the record failed I was in debt. If it hit, wouldn't everything go all haywire? Could I finish school? What if only *one* was a hit after our lives were changed around? You can see my problem. Finally I decided I'd finish school whether the record was a hit or not, but that I still had to follow my talent where it led and not be afraid of change.

So I borrowed the money, went to Chicago and we recorded *Two Hearts, Two Kisses*. It was a hit! Then I was asked to move to New York. That was a bigger step than Chicago, but I figured I could attend Columbia, something I wanted to do. And everything seemed to fall into place when Arthur Godfrey invited me to be on his show any time school permitted. I was out of a rut and into a life that certainly absorbed the biggest effort I had to give.

I was interested in what Conrad Hilton, Mr. Hotel himself, had to say in his autobiography (*Be My Guest*, Prentice-Hall, Inc.) about this point in following your own particular talent: Mr. Hilton thinks that finding it is the *first step in the art of successful living* and advises us not to worry if it takes a little time or chance, or change, to arrive at our own niche. Then he says: "This is no invitation to become a drifter, a professional malcontent. But every man has a right, a duty I would say, to search humbly and prayerfully for the place where he fits into the Divine pattern. I am encouraging boldness because the danger of our seniority and pension plans tempts young people to settle in a rut named Security rather than find his own rainbow."

And we teen-agers must find and follow our own rainbow!

A word about financial security

Do you know what I think money is? I think it's a convenient, useful symbol of gratitude. Of itself it's just special paper and special ink and special ways of designing little round metal discs. It has value only because we use it as a token of our appreciation for services rendered. You buy a head of lettuce at the store and you pay the man so many little round coins. Actually, you are repaying the service of a farmer, a trucker, a grocer, and probably a lot of other people who are quietly fulfilling their talent in the scheme of the great whole. We could change the symbol tomorrow back to nuggets or gold dust or wampum or pieces of eight. So in and of itself money can't be a goal.

Now, I like money. I really do. I like it because it's gratitude I earned from someone for my services and I can use it to pass on as my symbol of gratitude. Why do you get paid for baby sitting, or mowing a lawn, or doing a neighbor's ironing? Because you render a service and you don't want to be paid off in orange marmalade or angel food cakes. Or old Pat Boone records.

So the first step in financial security is to develop our talents until we can render a service so well that people will be very grateful for it. What happens if you, as a baby sitter, fall asleep and the parents come home and find the little cherubs have been up having a pillow fight? You've really messed up your financial security! But if you stay awake and wash the dishes as well, an extra service, you either get extra gratitude in the usual legal form, or you get a real steady type job. You see, they're extra grateful.

If you're not getting enough, try giving a little more.

That's the best and happiest way I know to earn. It goes without saying that if you get money for which no service has been performed, even if you are inside the legal law, you are outside the law of gratitude and this so-called "easy money" has a way of disrupting things.

All right, so now we've got money. The next step is how do we distribute it? I myself believe in a three point distribution program that was good at fourteen, is still good at twenty-four, and I see no reason why it shouldn't be good at ninety-four. To me all three points are of equal importance.

ONE: *You pay your bills.* You cannot expect others to be prompt with their symbols of gratitude to you if you're happy-go-lucky in remembering the gratitude you owe. I remember seeing a kinda sad little sign in a corner grocery store once:

> Some pay before due—
> Some pay when due—
> Some pay when past due—
> Some never do.
> How do you do?

Don't borrow beyond your means to repay—and this includes installment buying. It's a great thing. Shirley and I depended on it a lot when we were first married. But the guy who falls for every little gadget whether he needs it or not, simply because it's shiny and new and the payments are small, is building up to a big crash. We have to be wise about our spending.

Robert Louis Stevenson wrote: "Benjamin Franklin went through life an altered man because he once paid too dearly for a penny whistle. My concern springs from a deeper source, to wit, from having bought a penny whistle when I did not want one." Teen-agers, with their own money in their pockets, can get sidetracked buying "penny whistles" that they don't need, can't afford, and probably don't want anyway, and it's a hard habit to get rid of.

Two: *You share what you have* by supporting things like churches and charities and other worthy services that do not send bills to people. Just because they don't bill us doesn't mean we have no need to express our gratitude in concrete form. God has given you everything you have, and He asks in return only that you contribute according to your gratitude. A free school for the blind will never charge you, but you can share your gratitude for your own eyesight by helping someone who's deprived of it to lead a normal life.

In some way we are all receiving free gifts and we need to put something in if we are to continue to take out. It is a little like the preacher who traveled around the countryside during the summer speaking in various churches where the regular minister was on vacation. He depended for his living on the generosity of the people. One day he rode forty miles with his son to a small church and, as they entered, he dropped a quarter into a box set aside to help the poor. After the services a member of the congregation brought him the poor box. "We give the contents as payment to our visiting ministers," the man explained.

Inside, all alone, lay his own quarter. His son looked at it sadly: "Looks like you shoulda put more in, Pop," he said.

THREE: *You save and invest.* Remember, we said when we were making our maturity chart, that work and money were the freedom twins. Farmers do not sell their entire output. Ten percent of their best seed is returned to the land to sow a new crop. A certain percentage of what comes to us should be put to work for us so that we will always be in a position to back ourselves or others in a new venture, or so that, when a time of enforced idleness comes, we'll have stored up some gratitude and not need to mortgage our future.

Fifty years ago these business details were entirely the concern of the male animal. But today over half of the wealth in our country is in the hands of women. It is the housewife, in many instances, who pays the bills, saves, and shares. So the teen-age girl today has a real responsibility to understand the distribution of money.

And there, in a few thousand words, I've outlined my ideas on how to find your personal gold mine, how to work it, and what to do after it starts to pay. I've spent a lot of time on it, but just between you and me, it's really a major teen-age issue and responsibility.

I'll polish this off with a few words which are not original with me, but which I could sincerely say to you. Actually they were said by the famous English writer, Rudyard Kipling, to a group of students: "If you will let me, I wish you in the future what all men desire—enough work to do, and enough strength to do your work."

And that, my friend, from someone who knows (me!) is a cornerstone for a happy life.

9

Habit Weaving

Do you know what the largest room in the world is?

The room for improvement! (Ouch!)

It's the truth, though. Some grown-ups seem inclined to think that with a few well chosen words from them we are automatically improved. But in my personal experience no improvement was permanent until it became so much a part of me as to be almost automatic—in other words, *a habit!*

Habits, they say, are first like cobwebs, then like cables. Every time you repeat a set pattern you weave another strand for the cable. I don't know why it is so, but good habits seem hard to make, while bad habits are easy to make and hard to break.

I told you earlier about how I slid into time-debt. One result of this was that I was constantly rushing but still always late. The truth was that I had been a-weavin' that cobweb for years. Being late was a habit I sort of acquired somehow. Even in high school when I was riding the bus I can remember running like mad to catch it when basketball practice was over in the afternoon. I seemed to have a hundred loose ends, and by the time I tied them all, I'd have to fly across the campus with a big load of books and jump nimbly over the chain that marked one side of the driveway.

But somehow I always forgot to jump the second chain and there I'd be sprawled on the grass, surrounded by books and papers, watching the bus leave without me.

In fact I wove so many little strands of tardiness that the big fat cable continues to trip me to this day. After Cherry arrived, when we were struggling along in Denton, Texas, Shirley and I wanted a TV set the very worst way. Suddenly, I had a chance to make $75 from one personal appearance. This would pay for a second-hand set we'd seen at the local Western Auto Store. I appeared, however, just thirty minutes late and someone else had filled in for me—and also got paid for me. I'll never forget the look on Shirley's face when I told her.

It isn't that I'm a "wheelbarrow" type waiting around to be pushed. Nor, unhappily, can I claim to be on a par with Sir Winston Churchill, who, always pressed for time to keep his many appointments, sometimes misses trains, boats, planes and the like. Asked why this happened, Sir Winston replied: "I'm a sporting man, my boy. I always give them a fair chance to get away."

No excuse. I just got into the dull, annoying habit of being late. Now, if it weren't for Shirley and Jack Spina, I might never catch up with myself at all! Funny, too, knowing it, admitting it, trying hard to change it, there isn't anything else I know that really gets my goat except somebody fussing at me for being late. I arrive thoroughly disgusted with myself, and nothing anyone says could make me feel worse, nor could it possibly be any more severe than what I've just been saying to myself.

You get the point, I know. It takes more time to cut the cable than to weave it. The idea is to start young (at just about *your* age) and develop the habits you want. Ev'ry little thing counts!

Up to the teen age we acquire habits via the persuasion selected by our parents (the sewing machine strap, etc.), or by observation and imitation. We observe a lot and we pick up fast, too, both good patterns and bad. One five-year-old boy had acquired the powder-baby's-bottom habit before he'd ever changed a diaper just by watching his mother change little brother. This was apparent one day when mom, in a hurry, neglected the powder and was sharply reproved by junior: "Hey, Mom," he said, "you forgot to salt him this time!"

But when we arrive at the teen age, while we still observe and imitate, we can also begin to reason and choose the habits we want for ourselves.

To be or not to be?

We've already discussed quite a lot of habits and how they may be acquired or defeated—the "tomorrow" habit versus Jam Today, study habits, the art of listening, good manners.

Listening, the art of controlling my body so I could focus my mind, acquired so painfully during my early days in church, was a lifesaver after we moved to New York. There, I was attending Columbia and with a pretty full TV and work schedule. I had to alter my study habits to suit the schedule, catch up at the last minute, drag books around with me and do my work on buses, in cabs, over a ham sandwich at a lunch counter, at odd moments on stage during rehearsal. I couldn't have made the grade this way except for one thing. I depended heavily on what I learned in class. I didn't dare miss a lecture, or a word the prof said. And I'll tell you for sure that I could *not*, all of a sudden because I needed it, have developed the ability to concentrate, listen, and remember what it had taken me years and several lickings to acquire earlier.

Our manners, too, our automatic please-thank-you-hold-the-door-for-a-lady-cover-my-mouth-when-I-sneeze, have become pretty well grooved by now, or should have, because since we are teen-agers, people take a dim view of any such omissions on our part and we find ourselves in about the position of the poor guy who wrote:

I sneezed a sneeze into the air;
It fell to the ground I knew not where
But cold and hard were the looks of those
In whose vicinity I snooze.

When you begin now to choose the other assets you'd like as permanent parts of your personality make-up you will have to be deliberate about it at first. Think about it, put them on your maturity check list and then consciously make the effort to enforce them. Remember, don't pile up too staggering a load at first or you'll get tired just thinking about it. Easy does it, but *do* it! When you have worked at a selected few until they are habitual, then, and then only, they belong to you. At this point go on to the next ones.

The list is to be yours, personal to you. Mine were very personal to me, usually based on traits I admired in other people or positive good habits to overcome obvious flaws in my make-up, as with *Promptness*.

I've already admitted I haven't got this made, but think how much worse I might be if I didn't keep plugging away! Because of the trouble I've had, I—oh, so strongly—recommend that you get a good early start. That's half the battle and pretty well applies to the whole list.

It's like the story of the American tourist who admired the beautiful grass in London's Kensington Gardens. "How do you ever get lawns as perfect as these?" she asked the head gardener. "Well, madam," he answered, "the first thing you have to do is begin about six hundred years ago."

When you see someone who has developed perfect poise, or perfect promptness, or consistent gratitude, they usually began quite a time back. (Or else they were born with it. You *do* seem to get some of them just handed to you.)

It's a funny thing but one of the traits I value most is usually listed under "Education." It's reading! You hear people say today, "My child can't read," or you read an article about our "generation which hasn't learned to read." But I just don't believe it. I've asked some of the very ones accused (and they weren't all in grammar school, either) and y'know what? They know that C-A-T spells cat, and D-O-G spells dog and most of them can even figure out D-I-S-E-S-T-A-B-L-I-S-H-M-E-N-T-A-R-I-A-N-I-S-M. They can read all right. What they haven't developed is the reading habit. That's a question of practice.

And what a habit to overlook! Here, with a little extra effort on our part we can weave a cable that links us with every great adventure, every great personality, every great play, every great thought and invention, every land, every people. It can satisfy our curiosities, introduce us into any point of time—the past, the present, even into dreams of the future via science fiction.

For the girl or guy who develops the reading habit, the whole world, all periods and times and people, all animals, plants, the bottom of the ocean, the story of the heavens, all these things are there for the asking even if they never leave the small town in which they were born.

There is an old proverb that says "Man is himself—plus the books he reads."

Let me ask you, do you like music? Any of it? Pops, western, marches, rock 'n roll, tailgate Dixie, opera, symphonies, bagpipes—there's a lot to choose from, isn't there? Have any of the songs or instrumentals or jazz tunes or great inspirational music got you? I'll just bet that something has. And that something in music that you like has made your life a little richer, a little happier, a little fuller.

Now, do you like pictures? Moving pictures, dramatic news pictures, sports photos, fashions, portraits, candids of people you admire, cartoons that make you laugh, paintings of sea, land, boats, animals, children, flowers, trees, folks? If you do, then you know that, as with music, this visual art opens new worlds for you.

Believe me, the world of books is another miraculous

world. Once again it's a feast with something for every taste. Do you like adventure? Romance? Comedy? Travel? Mystery? Biography? Hobby material? History? It goes on and on. Among the greatest adventures I know, as you start acquiring this habit, are trips to the library. And one of the most exciting friends you'll make is the librarian, who is there right now, interested in *you*, waiting for *you*. She (or he) has spent a lot of time training to be your personal guide into the treasures of this particular gold mine.

Thomas B. Macaulay, the famous English statesman and writer, once said, "I would rather be a poor man in a garret with plenty of books than a king that did not love reading." (I, myself, would add "a phonograph and plenty of records" but since Macaulay was dead some thirty years before Edison got around to the phonograph, he didn't know what he was missing.)

At any rate, you might consider the eminent Englishman's statement extravagant at this minute, but you won't tomorrow if you begin to acquire the reading habit along with your listening and viewing habits.

Some older people might call the development of these things "culture," but for me, I'd put it more simply. It's part of the art of enjoying life, man! All we need to do is get with it!

Did you ever think of honesty and sincerity as habits? Well, they are. Real fine ones.

Deceit and untruthfulness, whether with ourselves or others, begin to operate just like the old-fashioned tongue twister. Each time we repeat the offense we get more and more mixed up, and farther and farther from the straight line.

Here, try saying over and over—"Tim, the Thin Twin Tinsmith." Then—"Six Slippery Sliding Snakes." Or—"Rubber Baby Buggy Bumpers."

You see what I mean? Well, that's just how you get mixed

up with any of the opposites of honesty. You start out all right but it gets worse the farther you go. Dishonesty, lying, deceit, they're all life-twisters. The answer is to practice honesty so that we'll be going straight all the time.

When I think about sincerity I think maybe one of the reasons I have always worked so hard toward having it in my personal make-up, is that there is one form of insincerity, that to me is pretty hard to take. But if you take enough of it, it seems to be as habit forming as a narcotic.

What is it? Well, what is it that makes everybody sick but those who swallow it?

Give up?

In a word, Flattery!

Honest praise and kind words are two of the finest things I know. That's why, I guess, I hate to see them caricatured by insincerity.

Thoughtfulness, consideration of others, to be consistently kind (there I go again! But you can't say I'M not consistent about kindness) must become habits or we are as uneven in our performance as a Vanguard test rocket. You never can tell until after the countdown what we'll do. This applies to little things as well as big ones, you know, even such little ones as this poor fellow had on his mind when he wrote:

> I wish I was a kangaroo,
> Despite his funny stance;
> I'd have a place to put the junk
> My girl brings to the dance.

Now you must know what it would cost a man to be the kind of kangaroo that has a pouch! And lest you think that I'm being hard on the fair sex in this matter I'll humble myself with a companion verse obviously written by one of the most humble of the ladies themselves:

> Women's faults are many,
> Men have only two—

> Everything they say
> And everything they do.

There now, that ought to cover it! That's why we have to work so hard at growing up.

Cheerfulness, neatness, humility, generosity, all those things we admire as virtues, are just something we admire until we put them into practice in our own lives and make them our own "second nature." It isn't possible to go down the list of all the attractive habits you may choose to develop as teen-agers. It isn't necessary either. You don't need to have them spelled out. I know that from your letters. But there is one last item I would like to add because it has been pretty valuable to me personally. I suppose there are more gentle and polite ways of saying it, but I was very blunt with me. I just called it the habit of minding my own business.

It's a full time job, to begin with, for me to keep in line and moving forward. And I found this habit, faithfully cultivated, kept me out of a lot of unnecessary difficulties. By it I meant all the usual things like not eavesdropping, not reading the notes other people passed in study hall, not being gossipy or nosey. It meant a little more than that, though, because I tried not to be prying or pushy or let my curiosity about what someone else was doing or what his home life was like, or what punishment he was going to get for breaking a rule—cloud my own defects and purposes. If tempted I could always remember what happened to Little Willie:

> Willie saw some dynamite,
> Couldn't understand it quite,
> Curiosity never pays;
> It rained Willie seven days.

So far we have certainly been thinking positively about habits. There isn't much question as to whether it's desirable to be prompt, thoughtful, sincere, and so on. But there are others that are obviously not desirable.

They say: "Habits are either bobs or sinkers, cork or lead. They hold you up or they hold you down."

Have you ever known grown-ups who click their false teeth? It's an annoying habit. Or teen-agers who snuff and won't blow? I hate to mention it and I know it couldn't be you, but I'm illustrating nervous habits because they are definitely sinkers.

Then there's the swearing habit. It's not only truly insulting to religious people (it violates both the Law of Moses and the teachings of Christ) but it's a symptom of character flaws. Swearing, or foul language, usually starts as an imitation (let's face it, all too often of some adult) and appeals to the eleven-year- or twelve-year-old as smart or grown-up. But it becomes habit through sheer laziness.

Did you ever hear the line: "He knew not what to say and so he swore?" To me that's pretty accurate about most offensive teen-age language. You have to use the ol' think piece more to say "That was a great quarter-back sneak" than "What a h— of a play." Bad language is a dead give-away that the user is covering up ignorance (he doesn't know what he's talking about) or is pretty lazy (he knows, but he won't take the trouble to say it). Or, worst of all, that he thinks it's smart! Which indicates very little "smart" on his part. Very rarely do these youths either realize or *mean* what they say.

The same applies to the ladies (we'll assume ladies never develop the above mentioned habit—I hope—I hope!!) who use terms of endearment so often that when they say "darling," you can't tell whether they are referring to their steady, their pug dog, a purple sweater, or the girl they can't stand! It's better to take your chances on a nice original "fluff," like those radio gems of Ken Allyn's—"Visit your nearest A and Poo Feed Store"; or André Baruch's "Good evening, ladies and gentlemen of the audio radiance!" than to get stuck in the "d—" and "darling" rut.

These habits are definitely not cork but lead. You can spot

them easily. And now we come to a couple of decisions that
face us all before we are out of the teen age. *Are we going to
smoke? Are we going to drink?*

The first real impulse to smoke usually hits around fourteen or fifteen when we are crazy-wild to appear older. Both
Shirley's parents smoked. Neither of mine did. Yet they handled us identically. "If you are going to smoke, and we
strongly advise against it, please do it here at home and *don't
sneak.*" I think it takes a lot of the excitement out of those
first cigarettes (and they're pretty hard to take at best) if
they aren't forbidden fruit. Then you can concentrate on
deciding, as a free citizen, whether you wish to acquire this
habit or not.

Shirley and I both decided against it. Her reasons were
that it wasn't very attractive, and it wasn't feminine. Mine,
at first, were partially that I was interested in sports and that
none of the people I liked and admired most (and whose
admiration and respect I desired) smoked. But later on,
when I started college, I did a little detective work on the
smoking habit.

Of all the habits I've heard about, smoking seems to be
one of the toughest to break. My suggestion is that before
you go into the experimental stage you do a research project
of your own on tobacco and nicotine (you can put it on your
health chart after you've mastered the art of the bath!). Go
to an authority, your science teacher (even if he smokes), a
medical man (your family doctor would be ideal) and ask
questions. I'll tell you now you'll get some astonishing answers. I know them already, but I don't want to spoil your
surprises! Just one fact: there are more than fifteen deadly
poisons and acids in every cigarette! Enjoy yourself!

When you've done this you'll have some facts upon which
to base your decision. Then you'll want expert opinions and
for you to get these I'd advise asking any ten adults who've
smoked cigarettes for ten years or more, whether they would
begin to smoke or not if they were your age and had a chance

to make their choice a second time. I'll give you a hint here. If a single one says "sure I would!" I'll eat a cigar! (A candy one, maybe.)

Anyhow, armed with facts plus expert opinions you should be able to make an intelligent choice based on something a little more lasting and solid than wanting to appear older or copy some adult.

So we come to the question of drinking. I personally don't drink. That was my choice. As with cigarettes, the law tries to protect you from the use of alcohol until you are old enough to have done some thinking on which to base a choice. The very fact that the government prohibits these things for young folks is enough warning for me. The human body doesn't change that radically when you've blown out twenty-one candles on your birthday cake! I'll brief the three reasons that led me to decide against it. These may give you some ideas for investigations of your own.

First, let me say that I tried drinking a couple of times. I've told you I was no saint. We were seniors in high school and we sent an older buddy out for beer. We thought we were real clever and had accomplished something. But the second time one of the crowd, a real nice smart guy, had one-too-many, or something, because right there in front of our eyes he turned into a real first rate zombi. It was like watching a Boris Karloff movie! I began to do a little more watching and came to the conclusion that I didn't want to take any chances of being transformed. If I have to be any part of a horse, I want to be the head! That was reason number one.

Reason number two was that I ran across some statistics. You can do the same at your local jail house. These were that out of 104,000 admissions to the jail in a big city in one calendar year 90,000 of them were connected with alcohol: (1) intoxication and cars (deadly combination) (2) intoxication and public nuisances (I can be enough of a nuisance without help from a jug) and (3) what is called "common drunk" (who, me?) vagrancy. And guess what? They weren't all tired old adults or Skid Row bums by a long shot. If you can engineer a trip to the drunk tank or get a look at some of the cars where a character tried to mix drinking and driving, you might decide you'd rather do without the stuff and sleep at home in bed!

At any rate, observation and investigation will give you something to ponder over before you begin spinning cobwebs of alcohol.

My third reason is one that I've had to think of in connection with all my habits and actions. It's a rule of thumb on which I try to base all my decisions.

The question that lights my life

When I used to go to Mack Craig with all those early problems and choices he'd say: "Forget what it means to you personally, or what you gain by it, or have to give up, or what someone else might think of it. Just ask yourself: 'Is it right?' "

When you look at life from that perspective the decisions aren't so hard and you always feel relieved. Of course, putting it into practice is what "ain't easy." But you know, we none of us can make our decisions strictly for ourselves. We talked a while back about people who "glow" for others. Well, I believe that every one of us has some influence, some chance to "glow" for someone else.

You think it sounds ridiculous that a lil ol' teen-ager has influence over other people's lives? Remember the Christian girl Bob Richards met? Look around you. Sometimes older brothers and sisters (even when they don't want it) have terrific influence over the younger members of their family as examples. You, personally, have influence over at least one person and probably a lot more than you realize.

And that means a double responsibility. To yourself and to the people for whom you "glow."

Now, maybe I could drink and handle my liquor like a

gentleman. I like to think I could. But I also believe that if my drinking influenced anyone else to drink, and they turned out to be the kind that couldn't handle it, I'd have my share of the responsibility. That alone would be a good enough reason for me. I know about alcoholics. Just from looking around me I know about drunken parents, tipsy parents, the whole lot. And I know you can't get into that kind of trouble if you never take a drink.

Well, that answers, for me, my question "Is it right?" The hard part is to stand on the answer.

Before we got the TV show we liked we had several tempting offers. One came from a cigarette sponsor. As I told you, I don't smoke, and so it would be hypocrisy for me to ask others, especially teen-agers, to smoke. I couldn't feel honest about it, that's all. But I wanted that show. So I asked the sponsor:

"Suppose I went before the camera, and said: 'I don't smoke. I don't advise you to smoke, but if you're going to smoke, smoke this brand.' "

They laughed and then said: "Why, that's a new approach. Maybe we ought to try it." They were getting serious, so we cut it off quickly. But do you see what I mean? I always try to ask myself about anything I do—

Will it violate my conscience?

Will it have a bad effect on others?

Will it have a good effect on others?

I'm not always sure about these things, but I try to be. That's basically how I want to select or reject the patterns that become habits in my actions. One of the chief reasons I try hard to live up to this, is *you*. I owe you a lot. You've helped me be a singer, and a success. I'm grateful. The only way I can repay you is to try everyday, to answer head-on and honestly the question that lights my life: "Is it right?"

10

God Is Real

Way back in the beginning of our talks I told you that I think our whole future, our sense of identity and purpose center around our faith. For me, God is not only the center of the entire universe, but the center of my personal life.

A soldier in the trenches once said: "True religion is betting your life there is a God." Well then, I'm betting on a sure thing because God is so very real to me that I could no more doubt His existence than I can doubt my own.

Does it sound a little egotistical of me to say "My God is real," as if maybe yours isn't or mine is different or better? Did you think I was bragging back at the beginning when I said I knew how real He is first hand? Like maybe I had some special introduction?

If so, let's get that straight real quick because it isn't what I mean at all. What I mean is that during my trip through the teen age I got to know God in a more intimate, personal way than I ever had before. And you can do that too.

In fact, now is the hour! Somewhere 'twixt twelve and twenty some one big thing or a combination of smaller ones brings us to the place where we need our heavenly Father in a way we never did before. We need to know Him for real, as a dependable part of our everyday lives.

Maybe you already do. If so, haven't you found that this opens a wonderful way of life for you?

But maybe you don't. I get letters saying: "This religion stuff's all very easy for you. You were raised on it. But what about me?" As if I sort of got it all second-hand from my parents.

I want you to know that this isn't entirely so. My faith is my own. This has to be true of me, or you, or the President of the United States. A famous Scotch minister once wrote: "Every generation must do its own seeking and finding. The fathers having found is only the warrant for the children's search." I believe that.

Maybe parents can carry us a short way when we are very young, like the youngster who called his friend on the phone and said: "Now page four, problem six—what answer does *your* Dad get?" But pretty soon we have to get our own answers.

You cannot get to heaven on your parents' ticket. The best they can do is give you an opportunity, an example, tips along the way. The worst they can do is slow you down a bit in the beginning. Even non-believing parents can't stop you from eventually getting your own ticket. Either way you have to do the traveling yourself.

This is a serious journey—if we believe that it has to do with the purpose of our whole life. It doesn't take away from our fun. I, personally, have a whale of a good time livin'. Faith doesn't have to make us "goody-goody" or sissy. But it's bound to make each of us a person-with-a-purpose, and that's serious. So let's approach it very thoughtfully.

The teen-age search

Why is the teen age such an important time in our spiritual growth? Because usually we arrive with varied backgrounds that present varied problems. The backgrounds fall roughly into three groups. You can pretty well pick out the group you belong to.

Group Number One knows ABOUT God, and right there it pretty much stops. That's not much practical use or comfort, because it's possible to know about God the same way you know about geography. It's something in books, on maps, in pictures, some place some lecturer has been. But the midnight sun, orchids on trees in the Amazon, a tiny oasis in the midst of the Sahara aren't real to you unless you travel. They don't influence your daily thinking or conduct one bit.

Individuals in this group have often got attendance awards at church. They can name the Books of the Bible just as they can recite the States of the Union. They do a little homework, maybe five minutes of prayer in the morning and five minutes at night (a total of ten minutes out of the 1,440 minutes in every day—still a good deal more than most of us). If you ask them if they believe in God, they look hurt and say "of course." But then, if you ask me if I believe in the Einstein theory, I can say "yes" too (although just between you and me, I am not one of the twelve people in the world who understand it!).

Well, all this is better than nothing, isn't it? But not much better. Going to church doesn't necessarily make you a religious person any more than going to a garage makes you an automobile! Knowing about God is very different from knowing God. And somewhere in the teen age something usually comes up that cannot be solved by any facts about God. You need God Himself!

Group Number Two arrives in the early teens having

known and felt God as very real in every way during their
childhood; but now that faith is challenged.

As our horizons expand, the unquestioning faith of childhood gets questioned. This I know, for I myself belonged to
this group. The "wise guys" want to know how come you regard the Bible as an authority. At some point there are heated
discussions over how you can dedicate your life to something
you can't see, and will never see on this earth. The seed is
sown that maybe this is all a myth, that God and Santa Claus
are somehow related. You hear the words "coincidence" and
"evolution," and you wonder.

I remember very clearly something that happened when I
was twelve. Mama had taken me over to the Milford
Smiths for the afternoon—me and my brand new baseball
that I had paid for myself. Milford, Jr., and I pitched ball in
their back acre until I threw a wild curve that got away from
him. The ball vanished in the tall grass. For half an hour we
searched. No baseball. Then Mama called, "Time to go."
Feverishly we trampled that patch with no luck. Mama called
again, this time adding "right now" in that I-mean-business
voice. I yelled an explanation and she just repeated : "Right
now!" Suddenly I thought, "Why don't I pray?" So I shut my
eyes and said: "Please, God, help me find the ball," and when
I opened them I was looking right at it. I'll never forget that.

To me at twelve, this was a proof of God's reality and His
interest in my affairs. It was pretty special. Then at thirteen
I heard that word "coincidence," and began to wonder.

I don't think there's anything wrong with wondering. I've
known very fine, dedicated, religious people who knew moments of doubt when they were young. It's wonderful if we
can keep the faith of little children without ever asking
questions, but it isn't fatal to our spiritual life if we can't.
Actually, in searching out answers that satisfy us, we are getting to know Him better. The danger is that if we don't seek

answers and let the doubts grow, they can choke off our faith and we drift away from Him. The trick is to face the doubts right on the spot while they're still small, and, by our own effort, weed them out, root and all, by searching for the answers that we need as the questions come up. This is to grow into a personal knowledge of Him that can't be shaken.

The Third Group arrives at the teen age with very little knowledge, teaching, example, or encouragement; perhaps not even much apparent interest. But somewhere in here, either through trouble, or curiosity, or some person who "glows" for them, they begin to feel a need, or just to "doubt their doubts."

I remember overhearing two brothers one day sitting on a wall in deep discussion. They came from a non-religious home where there was a good deal of drinking and very little "glow" for kids. One was thirteen and the other eleven and the older one said to the younger: "Look, there ain't any God, just like there ain't any sky." The younger one looked solemnly up at the blue above him and said: "Okay. Then what *is* that up there that ain't?"

This is a leading question. But following the lead is entirely an inner matter, because it is within ourselves that we have to find Him. It just isn't any good to argue and debate. I've always got a kick out of the eminent **Dr. Jowett** of Oxford, who sent for a skeptical student.

"Young man," he said, "I am told that you cannot find God. Is that true?"

"Yes, sir," was the reply.

"Well, you will please find Him before eight o'clock tonight or get out of this college."

I doubt if he had much success, because the point here is that you can't *order* anyone to "go find God." God isn't lost. You can't go out looking for Him the way you do for Fido's old bone. It all happens inside us, both the beginning of the search, and those questions—Who am I? or Where am I going? or Does life have a meaning? or What about problems or heartaches which we cannot seem to handle alone, or fears and doubts? Then comes the search itself; and then the finding. All must happen within us. The Bible is our guide book, but more on that in a moment.

We *all* start our search with exactly the same equipment. It doesn't matter what our background is, whether we belong to Group One, Two, or Three, or whether we are among those fortunate ones who have always known and never questioned. Each of us has at his or her disposal identical means for finding God as the real center of life. First, there is our intellect, our mind or ability to think and reason; second, there is our heart, where we feel, where we experience love and joy, praise and gratitude; third, is our ability to pray, to communicate and talk with God; fourth, is the opportunity each of us has to try in our actions to keep His commandments and trust that He in turn will keep His promises. This is all the equipment we need, and it has been given to each of us.

Doubts and fears

In dealing with my own doubts and fears, the first thing that occurred to me was that we already accept a lot of forces that are invisible simply because we see evidence of them. If a stiff wind uproots a big tree, we don't deny the wind because we can't grab it, put it in a box or take a picture of it. I hate to think where you and I might be without the force of gravity, but I've never seen it. I've never seen the North Pole either, but I know if I hold a compass in my hand in Hollywood, California, or Leonia, New Jersey, the needle is irresistibly drawn toward it. And just so, a part of every person seems to be irresistibly drawn toward God. I see the evidence of His laws all around me.

The same instinct that draws the needle of our souls toward God seems to tell us that this mighty Force is a great and lov-

ing and good One, because it draws our troubles and problems to Him just as surely as gravity holds us right side up.
We seem to feel His perfect justice because we are "right
with the world" if we keep His laws, and pretty miserable if
we break them. This Power draws us all to some degree whether we are conscious of it yet or not—like the Afri-
can woman who had just heard her first Christian sermon
and, turning to her friend, said: "There now. I always told
you there ought to be a God like that."

Along with this instinct, we can also use our intelligence or
reason. I am told that some men of science claim to trace the
life of man back to a single cell, floating in water, and finally
earth back to a whirl of cosmic dust.

> A fire-mist and a planet,
> A crystal and a cell,
> A jelly-fish and a saurian,
> And caves where cavemen dwell.
>
> Then a sense of Love and Duty,
> And a face turned from the clod,
> Some call it Evolution
> And others—call it God.

Even if you could prove that man was once a cell and the
earth a bunch of dust—that cell and the dust came from somewhere, brother! It had to be created!

Is it sensible to you that this intricate, magnificent creation, this awesome universe, was an accident? Look at your
wrist watch. Could it have been made by accident? Would it
run by accident? It just didn't make sense to me when I
really thought about it. Now, I'll admit I'm no great brain or
scientific authority, but I have read a good bit and here's
what a very great chemist, Sir William Crookes, wrote: "I
cannot imagine the possibility of anyone with ordinary intelligence entertaining the least doubt as to the existence of a

God—a Law-Giver and a Life-Giver." Sir William is one of a tremendous host of brilliant scientists who have been worshipers of God.

In connecting this Law-Giver and Life-Giver with my personal existence, I have been taught, as a member of the Church of Christ, to use the Bible as my principal authority. But how did I come to accept the Bible as "gospel truth"? Why couldn't it be a collection of old myths? No sense being afraid to try to pull that weed, so I began to study the Bible as history. You know, it states a lot of historical facts. It proves accurate! I got interested in some of the great archeological finds (including the Dead Sea Scrolls) which year after year add to our factual background for the Bible . . . and the story of some of these "digs," I might add, is science fiction backwards, and terrific! May I suggest books by Werner Keller and Harry Rimmer? Fascinating, exciting!

Yes, history confirms the Bible, and so does science. Sir James Jeans, a very eminent British physicist, astronomer, and author wrote: "The tendency of modern physics is to resolve the whole material universe into waves and nothing but waves; these are waves of two kinds; bottled up waves which we call matter and unbottled waves which we call radiation or light. . . . These concepts reduce the whole universe to a world of light, potential and existent, so that the whole story of creation can be told with perfect accuracy and completeness in the six words, 'God said, Let there be light.' "

In the first book of the Bible, Genesis, Chapter One, we read: "And God said, Let there be light: and there was light." Try that on your science teacher!

Let's admit, however, that Bible language has to be read thoughtfully. We can find ourselves as mixed up as the little girl who told her mother that the Sunday text had been: "Don't be scared. You'll get your quilt," when actually it was "Fear not, thy Comforter will come." But careful study of the word of God as it comes to us in the Bible is very definitely one of the greatest ways for knowing Him, His will, His way, His laws, His promises, and His presence.

Right along with our natural instinct and our intelligence, our heart is a channel for knowing God. The heart—my heart at any rate—is always the part that wants to believe. It was my head that tried to get me mixed up. All I have to do to feel Him in my heart is to go outside on a beautiful clear night and stand alone under the stars. I can almost feel the earth spinning under my feet, and I realize that I'm standing on a gigantic radiant globe revolving in a steady orbit through empty space at a tremendous speed, one among millions and millions of planets. And I can feel that every one of them, and our earth, my wife, my babies, you, and my small self, are resting confidently "in His hands." At times like that I am so aware of Him that I talk to him aloud.

There is no room for doubt or fear!

Or I can take a small buttercup like the ones I sold by the highway in Nashville, or watch a mother bird and her nest of scrawny babies, and sense the miracle of it, the miracle of life itself, and feel God's tenderness and love and wisdom. The evidence is all around us!

I remember a story that impressed me very much about an intellectual, clever man who had been both a communist and an atheist. Then one day he was looking at his little daughter's ear, and he decided that nothing but God, a very real God, could have made anything so wondrous as the human ear. If that doesn't appeal to you, look instead at the lives lived by people who loved God, like those of Albert Schweitzer, Florence Nightingale, George Washington Carver (if you aren't familiar with them, ask your friend the librarian for a hand!), and perhaps lesser known but tremendously dedicated servants of God like David Lipscomb and A. M. Burton and Alexander Campbell, and you find your heart singing with praise at the heights that can be achieved in human lives where God is companion, guide, and friend.

Doubts and fears simply cannot last long if we challenge them actively with head and heart. And we can't be satisfied with just knowing about Him when we realize that He can and should be the magnetic force which provides the direction for every minute of living.

Prayer

The instinct to prayer seems to be another response to an irresistible force.

You let any human being get into enough of a jam and he will pray in some way. He will be driven to appeal to a power greater than himself. In the days of sailing ships one man remarked: "If you want to teach a man to pray, send him to sea (where they got into some pretty tight situations)." An army commander said that there are no atheists in the trenches. In a tight spot, the confirmed non-believer will pray as quickly as the devout church-goer. Whether you believe now or not, the day will come when you will pray! But often, this sudden urgent interest in God won't have a very lasting effect.

I remember hearing about an atheist and his believing friend who were arguing because the believer insisted the other must have prayed at some time. The atheist kept denying it. But finally he recalled a hunting trip in the Yukon when a blizzard had separated him from his party, guides, supplies, dogs, the works. For some days he wandered around, snow-blind, half frozen, starving. Finally, he said, he fell on his knees and asked God's help.

"Well," said his friend, "it looks like you got it."

"Got it nothing," said the other. "If an Indian guide hadn't come along just then, I'd have died."

This fellow really must have heard of the long arm of coincidence! This type of praying is called "foxhole" praying. It's an SOS and while it attempts to meet a momentary need, it doesn't get you much better acquainted with God. Don't misunderstand me. I think (and I can only tell you what I think), that God's children have a perfect right to pray for help with any problem or difficulty, no matter how great or small . . . but there are other kinds of prayer we shouldn't neglect if we really want to know Him.

The same is true for me about asking prayer. I myself believe we should ask what we have need of, just as we are taught in the Bible. We should ask for others as well—our families, our friends, our government, even our enemies. And the Bible promises the believing prayer will be answered. But right here a lot of folks get mixed up. If we don't get exactly what we ask for, we aren't sure we're getting through.

Just the other night my Number One daughter, Cherry, at the close of her prayer, said: "And dear God, could you please speak a little louder. I can't quite hear you!"

Sometimes we feel the same way. We ask, and ask, and wonder if we're getting an answer. But we forget that "yes" isn't the only answer possible.

An older boy was teasing a little fellow because he had prayed and prayed for a bicycle for Christmas. "An' you didn't get it," the older one jeered. "God didn't answer your prayer."

"He did so," said the little fellow stoutly. "He said 'No!' "

Sometimes He says "no" to us, or "maybe." "Maybe" can be almost as painful as "no" because it means waiting and we aren't very patient. As somebody said: "The trouble is that God's in no hurry and I am!" But we shouldn't be. Not if we really trust Him to know the right thing for us.

I remember when Shirley and I moved to Denton, I needed a job very badly. I prayed and prayed, and pounded on the doors of all the radio and TV stations in Fort Worth and Dallas with no results. One station, WBAP, I didn't try because it was the biggest and most unlikely to hire a semi-amateur. When I kept getting turned down, I finally approached WBAP. They hired me on the spot. That was a good deal of waiting, and I didn't like it much, but in the long run His plan was a lot better than mine! Bob Gould and Sid Smith and Mr. Cranston at WBAP were among the best friends I've ever had.

Yes, asking prayers are part of our relationship with our heavenly Father, and we can go to Him with anything, but we must always remember that He can answer us in those three ways. And we shouldn't stop with asking if we really want to know Him.

A very famous man long ago said: "Some people want to see God with their eyes as they see a cow and to love Him as they love their cow—they love their cow for the milk and cheese and profit it makes them." It's a horrifying thought that I could get God mixed up with Rosemary, or any other cow. But it isn't usually until about the teen age that we begin to expand our ideas on prayer.

Robert Young tells about the first signs of this he noticed in one of his daughters. He and his wife knelt to hear her evening prayers and Bob says it sounded more like a letter to Santa Claus. Suddenly she stopped, there was a silence, and then she finished in a very small voice, "And now, dear God, is there anything I could do for you?"

This is a part of "growing up" at prayer, when we begin to say, "What will You have me do? Show me Your way, not my will but Thine. Is there anything I can do for another of your children?" Like the young Samuel, who said, "Speak, Lord, thy servant heareth." Or like the young Solomon who asked for wisdom rather than wealth or power, and was rewarded by God with all three!

Then, too, there is the prayer of intention. At least, that's what I call it. Often it isn't even put into words. It's just a kind of conscious pointing of your needle toward Him, like the shoe shine boy who was muttering the alphabet while blacking a customer's shoes. "A-B-C-D-E-," he muttered happily, right on through "Z" and then back to the beginning. "What are you doing?" the man asked. "Praying," he said simply. "That doesn't sound like a prayer to me," the man shook his head. "No, sir," said the boy. "But you see, I don't know a lot of words so I'm just giving the letters to God and He can put them together." This isn't as much a joke as it appears. The Bible teaches us that God's Holy Spirit brings prayers that we cannot utter to His throne!

Spring Byington, whose joy of living comes across so strongly on our TV set, has a prayer of attention, too, that I think is great. She uses it during busy days on the set when she hasn't time to "stop and pray." Each morning she reminds herself that Christ said: "Behold, I stand at the door and knock." Throughout the day Mrs. Byington opens the door by saying occasionally, "Come in! Come in!"

All these, then, plus spontaneous prayers of thanksgiving and joy, can make God the real center of our daily living. You'll be amazed and delighted at what a different life it is!

The uses of adversity

Shakespeare said it! "Sweet are the uses of adversity." It's a hard saying, but the Bard has a habit of turning out right. The key word is "uses." Our troubles can spur us on to greater growth if we use them that way.

When Shirley's mother died, Shirley was not a member of the Church. Her sorrow and her loneliness and her nagging guilt about all the little kind things she might have done for her mother, loving things she might have said to her before she died, were wearing her down. Now right there Shirley could have added a big load of self-pity and stood in it. Instead we used to pray out loud together, and Shirley prayed alone too. She began to seek, and in the end she found her

Comforter and became a member of the Church of Christ.

I can remember disappointments that spurred me on to greater understanding, like the time in high school, after I'd worked for three years on Clean Up Committees and any other place I could, that I lost the election for student body president. I admit I'd been pointing toward that since my freshman year. Then suddenly I lost to a guy whose chief qualification was that he was an outstanding athlete. He was a carefree kind of guy who'd only been in school one year, and I couldn't see what value twenty-five points a game would be at the Council table.

It was a bitter blow, and I was tempted to feel that it was all pretty unjust. In fact, I recall discussing this very thing with God. Finally I was able to pray, without any resentment or bitterness, that he'd be a good student body president. The wounds were actually healed. Then, when school opened in the fall, it turned out he'd become ineligible because of something that had happened during the summer. Another election was held and I won, but I didn't feel any gloating triumph. I just felt genuinely sorry for the other guy. I think this defeat was a very necessary lesson for me to learn in case I had to handle success later on. I picked up some humility, and learned that my efforts weren't necessarily going to win any prizes unless they fitted His plans.

Temptations (known to us all, yes?) can strengthen our spiritual muscles if we use them to that purpose. For me there are five ways to resist temptation. All of them make you grow. First, you avoid it if you can. Second, you have to be alert (Watch! as it says in the Bible) so that nothing sneaks up on you. Third, you pray! Fourth, you try to feel God's presence to help you in any difficulty. Fifth, you study His Word in the Bible and listen to sermons and advice from people who have already overcome them.

There are people, too, who have used great handicaps and suffering to turn apparent defeats into great victories.

Faith and confidence, plus hard work, turned tragedy into victory for Glenn Cunningham. As a kid, Glenn was badly burned saving his brother from a schoolhouse fire. His legs received the worst burns and healed slowly, covered with stiff ugly scar tissue. For a while no one believed he would walk again. With infinite patience and faith he began teaching himself—working behind a plow—until he could take a few steps. Then walk. Then trot. The training was long and arduous. The scar tissue never disappeared from his legs. But Glenn Cunningham became one of the greatest milers who ever lived.

Helen Keller has been deaf, dumb, and blind from her second year. Before Helen Keller's time, deaf-mutes were considered to be mentally retarded, unteachable, little more than animals. Miss Keller, with the aid of a dedicated teacher, learned to "talk" and "hear," graduated from Radcliffe College, wrote books, was literally the savior of hundreds who, but for her, would have remained captive in a completely dark, silent, world such as you and I can't even imagine.

Yet do you know what she discovered in that strange and terrible world devoid of all the evidence open to you and me? Under conditions that would have pulverized most people? She discovered that "Optimism [looking at the right side] is the harmony between man's spirit and the spirit of God pronouncing His works good." This from a woman who is deaf, dumb and blind! Bro-o-other! No wonder they called her the Eighth Wonder of the World! It reminds me of the words of the Blind Plowman: "God made me blind so that my soul might see!"

The point isn't that we should become blind, but that we, having eyes, should see, too! Helen Keller's entire life has been centered on her love for God, and it has been a miracle of adversity made sweet through her uses of it.

Once a famous newspaperman said: "There are plenty of

people to do the possible; you can hire them at $200 per month. The prizes are for those who perform the impossible. If a thing can be done, experience and skill can do it. If a thing cannot be done, only faith can do it."

Helen Keller, by faith, did the impossible. There have been many others. We may one day be called on to do some great thing and faith will be our most valuable asset.

You may think I've attempted to preach a sermon to you. A lot of this may have sounded very familiar. But I promise you that what I've said comes from my own, very real, experience. I know that it is practical and essential. Sure, some will find it very hard to accept and actually put into practice.

But the thing I am trying to tell you—and it is hard to put it into words—is that to love God, to know His will and way as revealed in His Bible, and to feel loved by Him, is to set your compass for the journey through life on a true course. It ensures your safe passage, your destination, and the greatest of all Companions on your travels. That is why we say to our friends when it is time to part what I say to you now: "God go with you every step of the way."

11

Dreams Do Come True

Now it's good-bye—for a while! But only a short while. I'll be seeing you and singing to you right along, and it will have a new meaning for both of us because now we're real friends. We understand each other. Our Coke bottles are empty, the sun is going down, but we've covered a lot of territory together. Maybe we never got around to deciding all the things the Walrus wanted to know—"why the sea is boiling hot" or "whether pigs have wings"—but we've tried to hit the high spots on that great question: "What is Life all about?"

You know what I think about many things. And I know what you think, because your letters tell me, and your smiles when we see each other, and the records you choose when we meet—musically speaking. Yes, now we are friends. And tomorrow, or day after tomorrow, I'll be seeing you up here at the other end of the teen-age ladder in the world of Young Adults.

You know how, when you leave a good friend, just as you walk to the door, a hundred things crowd into your mind that you want to say at the last minute, that time when Mom and Dad say, "What can they possibly have left to talk about?" They've been together all afternoon!" Well, here I am standing at the door, and I still have a few things left to say.

The first one is, no matter what you hear to the contrary, look forward to getting up here into the adult world. It's fun to grow up! I have told you the truth as I see it right along, and I'm telling it now. There are adults who will say to you sadly: "Have the time of your life while you're young, because, when you grow up you'll have so many responsibilities and so much hard work that you'll never have any more fun."

Well, maybe this happened to them. But it can't happen to you if you make up your mind about it right now. I've just spent a good many weeks working with three other guys who have passed into the young adult class: Dick Sargent, Gary Crosby, and Tommy Sands. Matter of fact, Tommy had his twenty-first birthday while we were making *Mardi Gras*. And you can take it from me that we had a lot of fun. Sure, we worked hard. Sure, we have responsibilities (you can count mine!). But there were a lot of laughs on our set and I was almost sorry when the job was done.

Your objective is maturity in six major areas: Spiritual, Social, Mental, Physical, Financial, Work. That's full development of your potential. It doesn't say anything anywhere about hardening of the arteries that control your sense of humor, of laughter, of gaiety. In fact, if you start fretting and worrying and carrying that big burden, turning into an Old Fogey (and there are such things), you've lost your Jam Today, your sense of living now. Full development along all these lines will keep you young in heart, honest! Maturity is not a synonym for Old Age. It means making the most of everything at every age. And that's happy living.

You don't ever need to give up your zest for life, or even all those little impulsive things that add spice to it. Mack and Dottie Craig say that, next to love, a sense of humor has been the most important ingredient in their happy marriage.

Actually, as you gain adult freedom you can have *more* fun

if you're prepared for it. Take my own case. All my teen-age
life I thought it was goofy to eat dessert, the best part of any
meal, last. Well, now I don't a lot of times. I eat it first. I
know I will get all my health foods down. I can trust me. So
I always start with the best.

Jack Spina says the reason he agreed to become my man-
ager was not so much my voice but the fact that when we had
our first dinner together in a swank New York restaurant, I
ordered steak, French fries, spinach, and a *banana split first.*
Well, now I doubt if Mama would have liked that! But I do.

I also named our company Cooga Mooga, because I heard
a disc jockey say it once and I just liked the sound. It doesn't
mean a thing.

My friend Jerry Lewis has a great time being an adult. I
don't know anyone who works harder than Jerry, or who
takes those maturity areas more seriously; but you get Jerry
into a strange town and the first thing he goes looking for is
the ball field. He'll suit up with the players, go through in-
field and batting practice, knock himself out for fun. And
he's good at it, too!

If you've worked on your maturity check sheet, responsibility shouldn't be such a great surprise to you that it'll get
your life out of balance when you have a few more responsibilities up here in the adult world. If you've kept growing,
you should be willing to go on growing and you won't fall
into the trap that helps make Old Fogeys. You won't be
afraid to try something new. Your mind won't get closed and
frozen so that you can't think new thoughts. You won't lose
your wonder at life, or your ability to pretend and make believe.

I suppose some of the "responsible" adults who are so bur-
dened with their importance couldn't enter into their children's world for fear their dignity might slip, but I highly
recommend it.

In the house we rented this summer there was a huge
grand piano. Cherry would set the telephone book on the

music rack and play her own compositions by the hour. I was expected to sing along with her. I did, too. I enjoyed it, especially the Smith's section. Should I have been too busy with "matters of importance?" I don't think so.

Above all, you cannot find any phase of life a dead end if you hang onto your ability to dream! And to believe that dreams DO come true!

They do, you know. That's why it's important that we keep our sights high, that we don't waste "dream" time envisioning bad things, or petty things, or just plain silly ones. Dreams, the kind I mean, can be sort of like molds that we pour ourselves into; then, backed by effort and prayer, they can become actual realities.

I dreamed a lot, as I've already told you—of exploring, of being a doctor, of a family, of all the wonderful things that life could bring me. I can remember sitting out in our old barn when I was nineteen, milking Rosemary (shortly before she retired) and singing. It was winter and it got dark early and my singing would sound great to me in that cold clear air. It never has, in fact, sounded so good. And Rosemary liked it. So I would sing, and milk, and dream of how great it would be to be a real singer like Julius La Rosa on Arthur Godfrey's show, and live in New York, and go to Columbia, and make records.

Yes, I thought that would be the most perfect life imaginable—and the most impossible—for me, a teen-ager in battered jeans who had lost every singing contest in Nashville and was sitting in an old barn milking an old cow. Yet, two years later I was living in New York, singing on the Arthur Godfrey show, going to Columbia, and making records. And while I'm at it, let me tell you that nobody ever had a better friend than Arthur Godfrey.

Do you see what I mean? Our dreams are like the big star over the prow of a ship. They are the direction in which we point our lives. So you see how important it is that we make them worth while. They do have a way of coming true.

Do you know why they can come true?

Because we live in America!

I know we've all learned The American Creed in school; but it was a while before I stopped to think what it meant to say "I believe in the United States of America as a Government . . . established upon those principles of freedom, equality, justice and humanity for which American patriots sacrificed their lives and fortunes."

And I don't suppose one of us hasn't, either seriously or in fun, declaimed along with Patrick Henry: "I know not what course others may take, but as for me, give me liberty or give me death!" Yet I, for one, didn't reverence what he said very much until I understood what priceless commodities freedom and liberty are.

Without liberty, without freedom, equality, justice and humanity, we are dead even if we go on walking around. That's why it's worth fighting for. That's why the sacrifice of lives and fortunes. Try to imagine yourself without these gifts of our country that we take for granted. I mean try it right *now!*

You can't, can you?

Because without them we have no right to dream, to work, to achieve. We cease to be human beings and become robots of some sort.

But until we begin to think about this, our patriotism is a bit on the robot side, too. How many times have you put your hand over your heart, looked at the Stars and Stripes, and said: "I pledge allegiance to the flag of the United States of America and to the republic for which it stands, one nation under God, indivisible, with liberty and justice for all."? I know. I can't count 'em either. But an important part of my growing up was to begin to realize what this meant.

It means that every single one of us is free to choose, "under God," what we wish to do with our lives. It means we, you, me, your Aunt Minnie, the boy across the street, we are all free to live where we choose, say what we choose, write what we choose, worship as we choose, work as we choose, and we also have the all-American right to gripe. We can dream the biggest dream we can conceive and it can come true.

Isn't that something? Isn't that something great?

A very wise man, Henry Ward Beecher, said: "The real democratic American idea is not that every man shall be on a level with every other, but that everyone shall have liberty, without hindrance, to be what God made him."

Now, you know, and I know, that everything we've been discussing is based upon that democratic idea. But we also know that without law we have no freedom. You find that hard to believe? Well, try crossing a busy street intersection when the traffic signal's out of order. It's utter confusion and no one gets anyplace at all! The signal is what guarantees the rights of each individual. Laws, in a democracy, are made by the majority to ensure that everyone gets their opportunity without hindrance.

It's silly to be a jay-walker. It's easier, and safer, to cross at the signals. The laws of our land are our laws. We made 'em. Why break 'em? All right, we make mistakes. Then we change 'em. We're free to do that too. But it's up to us. The more we come to value our American freedoms as our All-American right "to be what God made us," the better citizens we'll be and therefore the better our government will be. We are our government, unless we sit back and "let George do it!" Day after tomorrow you'll be the maker of our laws as well as the guardian of our liberty.

Besides the laws of the land, there are other laws as well. There are the laws of nature which guarantee a harmonious universe, and, if kept, a sound digestion and a sound body. And beyond these are the moral laws, and the laws of God. If we keep them they are rules for a Happy Life, the road map we need for our journey. If we break them, we are out of harmony. We get lost.

Security lies in obeying all these laws. Once you understand what they are, and why they are, that instinct to rebel

dies away, and this, too, is one of the great things about growing up.

But remember, security is not a rut. Security is dreaming
your dreams, using your freedom, living your life *today* by
the rules of the land, of nature, of your conscience, of God.
Then you can follow the dictates of your heart without fear
for the past or the future.

I'm often asked if I'm not afraid because you all have
helped me to sudden success. "What if the bubble bursts?"
the fearful adults ask. Well, I'll tell you. If the time comes
when my usefulness as a singer is over, when whatever good
purpose I can serve is fulfilled, I have perfect confidence
that another useful path will open up and that I'll be prepared to follow it.

We don't have to hold on to yesterday's dream!

I've been able to fulfill my hopes of religious service right
along with my work. The Church of Christ does not "ordain"
ministers and we can share our strength and hope and faith
with each other as the elders of the individual congregations
see fit. And, as far as education is concerned, I've never lost
the dream that someday, when I have time to do it justice, I
can go back to college and get my master's degree.

I would enjoy teaching and if the "bubble bursts" that
could be my direction. I could even have one of your children in my class! To me, the ordinary teacher in the ordinary
high school in this country who is dedicated to his profession
is doing a fine job, maybe greater than some ministers or doctors (or singers?). A teacher who takes his or her work seriously—and a homemaker who does the same—are of vital,
indispensable importance to the world in which we live. They
are not expendable!

So, you see, you can go right on dreaming even after you
hit the world of the Young Adult. Have fun now. Jam Today!
Lay a solid foundation and step on up here into the adult
world tomorrow. I'll be waiting for you! And may all your
best dreams come true!